Speed, Agility and Quickness

for

HOCKEY

SAQ® Hockey

Alan Pearson and Sarah Naylor

A & C Black • London

Metric to Imperial conversions

1 centimetre (cm)	=	0.394 in
1 metre (m)	=	1.094 yd
1 kilometre (km)	=	1 093.6 yd
1 kilogram (kg)	=	2.205 lb

First published 2003 by
A & C Black (Publishers) Ltd
37 Soho Square, London W1D 3QZ
www.acblack.com

Acknowledgements

Cover photograph courtesy of Empics; all other photographs and illustrations courtesy of SAQ International.

Typeset in Photina
Printed and bound in Great Britain by Biddles Ltd, Guildford and Kings Lynn

Contents

Acknowledgements

A very big thank you to Leicester Ladies Hockey Club, Chris Mayer, Laura Lee, Emily Cotterill (and her Mum!). To David, Angus, Silvana and especially Alan at SAQ International for your continued advice, support and enthusiasm. Thanks also to Nike UK for their ongoing support.

A special thank you to Caroline Birt, Bo Koolen and Riet Kuper for your support and belief in the SAQ Hockey Programme.

Finally all my love to Mum, Dad, Jamie, Anna and Jo for your constant encouragement, support and understanding.

Sarah Naylor
2002

Forewords

Over the last 25 years hockey has changed more than any other team-sport. From natural (muddy) grass to the different types of artificial surfaces, new revolutions in stick materials and goalkeeping equipment and major changes in the rules that govern the game.

However with regard to the physical preparation of players for the 'new' sport, a change in attitude and approach has been very slow. When Alan Pearson introduced SAQ Training to Fyffe's Leicester I instantly knew that this was the way forward, the way to get my team ready for the changed physical demands of the game. Firstly, all drills are sports-specific, the leg speed, power, balance, nimble foot-work, acceleration and upper-body strength required by hockey players are all addressed. They can all be practised with or without a stick and ball!

Over the last couple of years I have introduced and used SAQ at all levels in the sport from juniors up to the seasoned premier (international) league player. The feedback I get from all the players is the same: it does make a big difference to their performance, and they enjoy the sessions. The enjoyment stems from the fact that there is enormous variety in the drills. Programmes can be tailor-made for both the individuals and the team, even if the fitness levels within the team are different.

SAQ Hockey covers all aspects needed for our fast and powerful sport and is the first book specifically written for it. I would like to say to you: 'Read it, work out a programme and introduce it to your players. You will see them get hooked on it.'

Bo Koolen
Hounslow & Ealing 1st coach
and Coaching Director
Southern Counties H.A. Coach and Adviser

In Ireland, our international rugby players have used SAQ methods for some time, so when the opportunity arose for the international hockey squad to experience a full SAQ session, we jumped at it.

There was an element of raw curiosity, a chance to see for ourselves what all the excitement was about. As coaches, we've all experienced the 'great new idea' syndrome. Within minutes it was clear that SAQ was different. From that day on, it was obvious that the physical side of our training would never be the same again.

For hockey coaches, SAQ offers an irresistible combination: injury prevention, increased power, improvements in speed and a structured method for players to develop rapid changes of direction under control. It's ideal for hockey, very game-related and offers enormous variety to keep our players interested.

The reaction to its introduction has been hugely positive, and I can safely say that players of all ages from junior school teams to senior international panellists have really enjoyed and benefited from the hockey-specific SAQ programme. I'd encourage anyone in hockey to try SAQ and hope that it will be as enjoyable and effective for you as it has been for the teams that I've been involved with.

Riet Kuper
FIH Supercoach
Coach to Irish Women's Hockey Team

In today's sporting environment, every athlete is looking for that extra something to give themselves the competitive edge. I found that edge – with SAQ.

I came to England, a young inexperienced international hockey player, desperate to succeed, but not sure how I was going to achieve that. My first training session was a shock to the system when our club coach pulled out mini-parachutes and bungee-like cords. I took one look at the tools, the exercises and what the coach said and thought: 'Not another crazy training idea.' Little did I know that such training would transform me from an average player into a class international.

Initial improvements were hard to see, as I continued to doubt that this SAQ training would make any difference to me. I remember looking at the ladder and thinking: 'Ladders are for climbing up and painting walls, not running through!' Today, the ladder has become an integral part of my training, testing both my brain and my feet to work out of their comfort zones. This is an invaluable piece of equipment for any hockey team – the benefits are simply astounding.

Playing in an incredibly competitive EHL, teams likely to succeed were the ones finding new ways to improve. Having begun our SAQ training programme in December, by February our club side had set new physical standards for women's teams in the EHL. We were stronger, fitter and faster, and were successful in winning the league because of our physical superiority. SAQ training brought that something new to our team, helping to make us successful.

Yes, the warm-up is different. And thank goodness for that! I am a trainer's nightmare, claiming that 'stretching is against my religion!' but with the dynamic flex warm-up, I found myself going into games ready from the onset, my body dying to get going. It is essential in my position as a goalkeeper to be able to react and explode around the goal area. With the standard running and static stretching warm-up, I found this impossible. With the SAQ warm-up however, I was ready from the word go, capable of making explosive saves that I had never made before.

I have to humble myself from those early days of negativity and admit that I wouldn't be where I am today without the contribution SAQ training has made to my hockey. Most players will agree that after time, training becomes monotonous and boring, but SAQ is dynamic, and allows for hundreds of different, valuable exercises, keeping your training fresh, challenging and fun.

I can finally say, after trying many different training methods and ideas, that I have found the perfect one – SAQ. If you are remotely serious about succeeding in the sport, get yourself some tools, get going and prepare yourself for new heights.

Caroline Birt
South Africa International

Introduction

The Foundation of SAQ for Hockey

There is an increasing need for hockey players to be not only highly skilled and tactically astute but also athletically adept. Today's game makes great physical demands on its players – picture the midfielder carrying the ball at speed towards an opponent, wrong-footing her and exploding into the gap created. The forward who cuts back towards the ball before stepping inside, turning and accelerating onto the ball played down the line, or the goalkeeper who saves from a penalty corner strike and gets to her feet in a dynamic, well-coordinated and balanced manner to make the second save. These are not isolated incidents that happen occasionally in a game – we would expect to see them again and again, and consequently there is an increasing demand on players to be able to perform such moves repeatedly.

The necessary qualities once thought to be predominantly genetic are in fact very trainable. All players from beginners and 'social' players to Internationals can be made faster, more agile, more explosive and ultimately better hockey players. *SAQ Hockey* introduces drills and programmes designed specifically with the physical needs of the hockey player in mind. Starting with the fundamentals before progressing through to not only hockey-specific but also position-specific drills, this book will show coaches and players how to develop the capability of repetitive, multi-directional, explosive speed and agility.

What is SAQ Training?

Speed, agility and quickness of hand, of response, of action are undoubtedly highly desirable in both team and individual sports. These qualities, that are inherited genetically in different proportions in different individuals, can also be trained and developed. The SAQ Hockey Programme aims to maximise each individual's potential in his or her genetically inherited abilities.

The SAQ Hockey Programme concentrates on developing movements – whether linear, lateral or vertical – that are automatic, explosive and precise, qualities that are required time and time again to wrong-foot an opponent and exploit the gap created, or, by a goalkeeper, to make a second-phase reaction save. Through continuous but precise repetition of the SAQ training drills, the neuromuscular link between intention and action is improved and imprinted. The result is a player who is able to react quickly and explosively whatever his or her playing position.

The more general exercises within the SAQ Hockey Programme are adapted, developed and progressed to incorporate the specific requirements of the game of hockey. Some of the drills concentrate on footwork, power and acceleration in different directions and situations. Others are more directly concerned with timing and hand–eye co-ordination to meet the needs of all players.

Speed

A crucial part of any player's game is the ability to cover the ground efficiently and economically over the first few yards and then to open up stride length and increase stride frequency when working over longer distances. Speed means the maximum velocity a player can achieve and maintain. In most humans the ability to maintain this maximum velocity is for a short period of time and distance only. Speed can also be measured by the amount of time it takes a player to cover a particular distance.

Training to improve maximum speed requires a great deal of focus on correct running mechanics, stride length and frequency, the leg cycle and hip height and position. Drills such as the 'dead-leg run' and stride frequency drills that are used to help develop an economical running technique can be easily integrated into a training session.

The best sprinters spend very little time in contact with the ground, and what contact they do make is extremely efficient and powerful. Focusing on the mechanics of running helps to control this power and to use it efficiently and sparingly. Training when fresh is also crucial for an athlete/player to attain maximum speed. Many athletes can only reproduce top speeds for a few weeks of the year, but the inclusion and practising of correct running mechanics on the training field will benefit players of the game greatly. How often do you see players holding the stick in both hands while chasing a ball, so that they run with a rowing-type arm action? Running with the stick in two hands will almost certainly create a rolling motion in the shoulders that will transfer through the core to the lower half of the body, resulting in a slower player. Failure to use good arm mechanics might make the difference between a player reaching the ball or not or missing an opportunity to pressure the opposition into making a mistake. Correct mechanics and overall running techniques are crucial in the development of explosive, balanced hockey players.

Agility

Agility is the ability to change direction without the loss of balance, strength, speed or body control. here is a direct link between improved agility and the development of an individual's timing, rhythm and movement.

Agility should not be taken for granted and can actually be taught to individual players. Training agility ensures that a hockey player develops the best attacking and defensive movement skills possible with the greatest quickness, speed and control and the least amount of wasted energy and movement. Agility also has many other benefits for the individual, helping to prevent niggling injuries and teaching the muscles how to fire properly and control minute shifts in ankle, knee, hip, back, shoulder and neck joints for the optimum body alignment. Imagine the type of agility a player requires to run at pace, drop the shoulder to wrong-foot the defender, sidestep and accelerate away without slowing down or losing control.

Another very important benefit is that agility training is long-lasting. Unlike speed, stamina and weight training, it does not have to be maintained to retain the benefits. Consider the elderly person who can still ride a bicycle 40 years after having last ridden one. Agility training acts like an indelible mark, programming muscle memory.

THE ELEMENTS OF AGILITY

There are four elements to agility:

- balance
- co-ordination
- programmed agility and
- random agility.

Within these there is speed, strength, timing and rhythm.

Balance is a foundation of athleticism. Here we teach the ability to stand, stop and walk by focusing on the centre of gravity; it can be taught and retained relatively quickly. Examples include: standing on one leg, walking on a balance beam, standing on a balance beam, standing on an agility disc, walking backwards with your eyes closed and jumping on a mini trampoline and then freezing. It does not take too long to train balance. It requires only a couple of minutes, two or three times a week with the emphasis placed early in the morning and early in a training session.

Co-ordination is the goal of mastering simple skills under more difficult stresses. Co-ordination work is often slow and methodical with an emphasis on correct biomechanics during athletically demanding movements. Training co-ordination can be completed by breaking a skill down into sections then gradually bringing them together. Activities include footwork drills, tumbling, rolling and jumping. More difficult examples are: walking on a balance beam while playing catch; running along a line while a partner lightly pulls and pushes in an attempt to move the player off the line; and jumping on and off an agility disc while holding a jelly ball.

The third element of agility training is called **programmed agility**. This is when a player has already experienced the skill or stress that is to be placed on him or her and is aware of the pattern and sequence of demands of that experience. In short, the player has already been programmed. Programmed agility drills can be conducted at high speeds but must be learnt at low, controlled speeds. Examples are zigzag runs, 4-corner ball and T cone drills, all of which involve a change in direction along a known, standardised pattern. Also the pattern of body height adjustment should be practised here, with drills focused on straight and angled runs where players have to drop their body height to simulate picking up the ball and making a pass before returning to a more upright position and reasserting the arm and foot mechanics needed for acceleration. Once these types of drills are learnt and performed on a regular basis, times and performances will improve and advances in strength, explosion, flexibility and body control will be witnessed. This is true of players of any ability.

The final element, the most difficult to master, prepare for and perform is **random agility**. Here the player performs tasks with unknown patterns and unknown demands. Here the coach can incorporate visual and audible reactive skills so that the player has to make split-second decisions with movements based upon the various stimuli. The skill level is now becoming much closer to that of an actual game. Random agility can be trained by games such as tag, read and react (tennis ball drops and dodge) and more specific training such as turning through 180° followed by an immediate unknown movement demand from the coach.

Agility training is challenging, fun and exciting. There is the opportunity for tremendous variety and training should not become boring or laborious. Agility is not just for those with elite sporting abilities – try navigating through a busy shopping mall!

Quickness

When a player accelerates, a great deal of force has to be generated and transferred through the foot to the ground. This action is similar to that of rolling up a towel (the 'leg'), holding one end in your hand, and flicking it out to achieve a cracking noise from the other end (the 'foot') – the act of acceleration in a fraction of a second that takes the body from a static to a dynamic position. Muscles actually lengthen and then shorten instantaneously, that is an 'eccentric' followed by a 'concentric' contraction. This process is known as the stretch shortening cycle (SCC) action. SAQ Training concentrates on improving the neuro-muscular system that impacts on this process, so that this initial movement – whether lateral, linear or vertical – is automatic, explosive and precise. The reaction time is the time it takes for the brain to receive and respond to a stimulus by sending a message to the muscle causing it to contract. It is what helps a forward explode through a gap or the goalkeeper make a dynamic diving save and then get to his or her feet to make a second-phase save. With ongoing SAQ Training, the neuro-muscular system is reprogrammed and restrictive mental blocks and thresholds are removed. Consequently messages from the brain have a clear path to the muscles so that the result is an instinctively quicker player.

Quickness training begins with 'innervation' (isolated fast contractions of an individual joint). For example, repeating the same explosive movement over a short period of time, such as in fast-feet and line drills. These quick, repetitive motions take the body through the gears, moving it in a co-ordinated manner to develop speed. Integrating quickness training throughout the year by using fast-feet and reaction-type drills will result in the muscles having increased firing rates. This makes players capable of faster, more controlled acceleration. The goal is to ensure that your players explode over the first 3–5 yards. Imagine that the firing between the nervous system and the muscles are the gears in a car, the timing, speed and smoothness of the gear-change means the wheels and thus the car accelerate away efficiently, with balance and co-ordination, so that the wheels do not spin and the car does not lose control.

Movement skills

Many elements of balance and co-ordination involve the processing of sensory information from within the body. Proprioceptors are sensors that detect muscular tension, tension in tendons, relative tension and pressure in the skin. In addition, the body has a range of other sensors that detect balance. The ability to express balance and co-ordination is highly dependent on the effectiveness of the body's internal sensors and proprioceptors, just like the suspension on a car. Through training, these sensors, and the neural communication system within the body become more effective. In addition, the brain becomes more able to interpret these messages and formulate the appropriate movement response. This physiological development underpins effective movement and future movement skill development.

SAQ Equipment

SAQ Equipment adds so much variety and stimulus to a training session. Drill variations are endless and, once mastered, quite astonishing results can be achieved. Players of all ages and abilities enjoy the challenges presented to them when training with SAQ Equipment, particularly when introduced in a hockey-specific manner.

When using SAQ Equipment, coaches, trainers and players must be aware of the safety issues involved and of the reduced effectiveness and potentially dangerous consequence of using inappropriate or inferior equipment. The following pages introduce a variety of SAQ Equipment recommended for use in many of the drills detailed later in this book.

FAST FOOT LADDERS

These are constructed of webbing with round, hard plastic rungs spaced approx. 18 inches apart; they come in sets of 2 sections each measuring 15 feet or 4 sections each measuring 7½ feet. The sections can be joined together or used as two separate ladders. They can also be folded over to create different angles for players to perform drills on. Fast Foot Ladders are good for improving agility and for the development of explosive fast feet.

MICRO AND MACRO V HURDLES

These come in two sizes: Micro V Hurdles measuring 7 inches and Macro V Hurdles measuring 12 inches in height. They are constructed of a hard plastic and have been specifically designed as a safe, free-standing piece of equipment. It is recommended that the hurdles be used in sets of 6–8 to perform the mechanics drills detailed later. They are ideal for practising running mechanics and low-impact plyometrics; the micro hurdles are also useful for lateral work.

SONIC CHUTE

These are constructed from webbing (the belt), nylon cord and a lightweight cloth 'chute', the size of which may vary from 5 to 6 feet. The belts have a release mechanism that drops the chute so that the player can explode forwards. These are effective for developing sprint endurance.

VIPER BELT

This is a resistance belt specially made for high-intensity training. It has three stainless-steel anchor points where a flexi-cord can be attached. The flexi-cord is made from surgical tubing with a specific elongation. The Viper Belt has a safety belt and safety fasteners, it is double stitched and provides a great level of resistance. This piece of equipment is good for developing explosive speed in all directions.

SIDE-STEPPERS

These are padded ankle straps that are connected together by an adjustable flexi-cord. They are useful for the development of lateral movements.

REACTION BALL

A rubber ball specifically shaped so that it bounces in unpredictable directions.

PUNCH/KICK RESISTER

A padded cuff that can be worn around the ankle or the wrist with a flexi-cord attached to it. Designed to provide resistance, particularly for punching and kicking development.

OVERSPEED TOW ROPE

The overspeed tow rope is made up of two belts and a 50-yard nylon cord pulley system. It can be used to provide resistance and is specifically designed for the development of express overspeed and swerve running.

BREAK-AWAY BELT

This is a webbing belt that is connected by Velcro-covered joining strips. It is good for mirror drills and position-specific marking drills, breaking apart when one player gets away from the other.

STRIDE FREQUENCY CANES

Plastic, 4-foot canes of different colours that are used to mark out stride patterns.

SPRINT SLED

A metal sled with a centre area to accommodate different weights and a running harness that is attached to the sledge by webbing straps of 8–10 yards in length.

JELLY BALLS

Round, soft rubber balls filled with a water-based jelly-like substance. They come in different weights from 2 to 8 kg. They differ from the old-fashioned medicine balls because they can be bounced with great force onto hard surfaces.

HAND WEIGHTS

Foam-covered weights each weighing 1·5–2·5 lb. They are safe and easy to use both indoors and outdoors.

VISUAL ACUITY RING

A hard plastic ring of about 30 inches in diameter with 4 different-coloured balls attached to it, equally distributed around the ring. It helps to develop visual acuity and tracking skills when thrown and caught between the players. This piece of equipment is particularly good for goalkeepers.

PERIPHERAL VISION STICK

The stick is simple but very effective for the training of peripheral vision. It is about 4 feet long with a brightly coloured ball at one end. Once again this is particularly good for goalkeepers.

BUNT BAT

A 4-foot stick with 3 coloured balls – one at each end and one in the middle. Working in pairs, one player holds the bat with two hands while the other throws a small ball or bean bag for the first player to 'bunt' or fend off. Useful for all players but particularly for goalkeepers' hand–eye co-ordination.

AGILITY DISC

An inflatable rubber disc 18 inches across; the discs are multi-purpose but particularly good for proprio-receptive and core development work. They can be stood, knelt, sat, and lain on for the performance of all types of exercises.

The SAQ Continuum

Team games such as hockey are characterised by explosive movements, acceleration and deceleration, agility, turning ability and speed of responses (Smythe 2000). The SAQ Continuum is the sequence and progression of components that make up a SAQ Training session. The progressive elements include hockey-specific patterns of running and drills including stick and ball work. The Continuum is also flexible and once the pre-season foundation work has been completed, during the season when time and recovery are of the essence short combination SAQ Training sessions provide a constant top-up to the skills that have already been learned.

SAQ Training is like any other fitness training, in that if it is neglected then players' explosive, multi-directional power will diminish. The component parts of the SAQ Continuum and how they relate to hockey are:

- **Dynamic Flex** – warm-up on the move involving hockey-specific movements
- **mechanics of movement** – the development of running form for hockey
- **innervation** – fast feet, agility, co-ordination and control for hockey
- **accumulation of potential** – the bringing together of the previous components in a SAQ Training hockey circuit
- **explosion** – the development of explosive 3-step multi-directional acceleration for hockey
- **expression of potential** – short competitive team games that prepare the players for the next level of training
- **warm-down**

Throughout the continuum, position-specific drills and skills can be implemented.

CHAPTER 1 DYNAMIC FLEX

WARM-UP ON THE MOVE

It is a known fact that, before engaging in intense or strenuous exercise, the body should be prepared. The warm-up should achieve a change in a number of physiological responses in order that the body can work safely and effectively:

- an increase in body – specifically core (deep) muscle – temperature
- an increase in heart rate and blood flow
- an increase in breathing rate and oxygen supply
- an increased level of activity and co-ordination in the neuro-muscular system
- an increased mental alertness

The warm-up should take one from a rested state to the heightened physiological state required to perform. It should gradually increase in intensity as the session goes on, and be specific to the numerous physical demands placed on a hockey player that differ from those involved in other sports.

What is Dynamic Flex?

Traditionally, warming-up for hockey has involved laps of the pitch followed by static stretching. Static stretching is not really relevant for hockey players as they warm up, because it does not replicate the movements that they are likely to perform in the next phase. They do not need to be able to perform the splits like a gymnast but they do need to be able to perform fast, agile movements in every direction.

Recent research has indicated that static stretching before training or competition can actually be detrimental to performance. The eccentric (lengthening) strength of the muscle, for example the hamstrings

as the player brakes quickly, was found to decrease by up to 9% within an hour of static stretching. Similarly, studies on the links between static stretching and injury prevention have brought into question the traditionally held belief that static stretching prior to intensive activity will decrease the risk of injury (Gleim and McHugh 1997). Similarly, an Australian Army physiotherapist (Pope 1999) studied army recruits over the course of a year. He instructed half to warm up with static stretching, and half to warm up without any stretching at all. He found no differences in the incidence of injury between the two groups, suggesting that static stretching is of little benefit in pre-exercise warm-up.

Dynamic Flex offers a fun, stimulating and – most importantly – an extremely effective alternative to the traditional approach. The standard SAQ Dynamic Flex session for hockey players begins with a series of low-intensity activities such as skipping. As players begin to get warmer, the drills become increasingly more intense with a greater range of movement more specific to hockey.

The warm-up

A standard 20×20 yard grid is used (*see* fig. 1.1). The following exercises represent a foundation set of Dynamic Flex warm-up drills. Also included in this chapter are variations and the introduction of the stick and ball.

It is important to remember that hockey players not only enjoy variety but also respond proactively on the field to variations in training. Once they have mastered the standard set, the introduction of new grids (*see* figs. 1.2–1.6) and combination work including the ball and stick will ensure maximum participation.

In a warm-up drill, start slowly, rehearse the movements then increase the intensity.

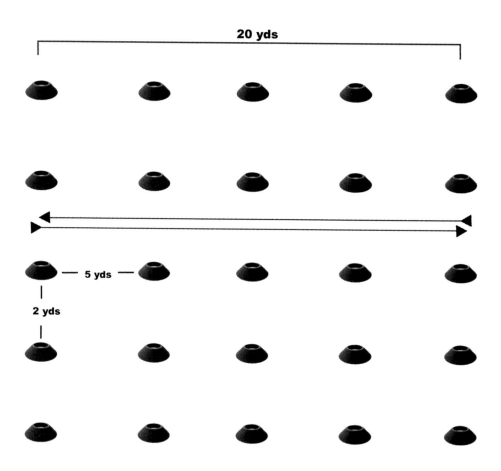

Figure 1.1 Standard grid

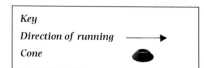

DRILL   *WALKING ON THE BALLS OF THE FEET*

Aim
To stretch shins and improve ankle mobility. To improve balance and co-ordination. To increase body temperature.

Area/equipment
An indoor or outdoor grid 20 yards long. The width of the grid is variable depending on the size of the squad (*see* fig. 1.1).

Description
The player is to cover the length of the grid by walking on the balls of the feet, and return to the start by repeating the drill backwards.

Key teaching points
- Do not walk on the toes
- Keep off the heels
- Maintain correct arm mechanics (*see* page 35)
- Maintain an upright posture

Sets and reps
2 × 20 yards, 1 forwards and 1 backwards.

Variations/progressions
Perform the drill laterally but do not allow the feet to come together completely. Push off with the back foot, do not pull with the lead foot.

DRILL ANKLE FLICKS

Aim

To stretch calves and improve ankle mobility. To improve balance, co-ordination and rhythm of movement. To prepare for good foot-to-ground contact. To increase body temperature.

Area/equipment

An indoor or outdoor grid 20 yards long. The width of the grid is variable depending on the size of the squad.

Description

The player is to cover the length of the grid in a skipping motion – the balls of the feet plant then flick up towards the shins. The player should be seen to move in a bouncing manner. Return to the start by repeating the drill backwards.

Key teaching points

- Work off the balls of the feet, not the toes
- Practise the first few steps on the spot before moving off
- Maintain correct arm mechanics (*see* page 35)
- Maintain an upright posture

Sets and reps

2 × 20 yards, 1 forwards and 1 backwards.

Variations/progressions

Perform the drill laterally.

DRILL SMALL SKIPS

Aim
To improve lower leg flexibility and ankle mobility. To improve balance, co-ordination and rhythm and develop positive foot-to-ground contact. To increase body temperature.

Area/equipment
An indoor or outdoor grid 20 yards long. The width of the grid is variable depending on the size of the squad.

Description
The player is to cover the length of the grid in a low skipping motion and return to the start by repeating the drill backwards.

Key teaching points
- Knee to be raised to an angle of about 45–55°
- Work off the balls of the feet
- Maintain correct arm mechanics (*see* page 35)
- Maintain an upright posture
- Maintain a good rhythm

Sets and reps
2 × 20 yards, 1 forwards and 1 backwards.

Variations/progressions
Perform the drill laterally.

DRILL KNEE-ACROSS SKIP

Aim
To improve outer hip flexibility and hip mobility over a period of time. To develop balance and co-ordination. To increase body temperature.

Area/equipment
An indoor or outdoor grid 20 yards long. The width of the grid is variable depending on the size of the squad.

Description
The player is to cover the length of the grid in a skipping motion where the knee comes across the body, and return to the start by repeating the drillbackwards.

Key teaching points
■ Do not force an increased range of motion (ROM)
■ Work off the balls of the feet
■ Maintain a strong core
■ Maintain an upright posture
■ Control the head by looking forwards at all times
■ Use the arms primarily for balance

Sets and reps
2 × 20 yards, 1 forwards and 1 backwards.

Variations/progressions
Perform the drill laterally.

DRILL   *KNEE-OUT SKIP*

Aim
To stretch the inner thigh and improve hip mobility. To develop an angled knee drive, balance, co-ordination and rhythm. To increase body temperature.

Area/equipment
An indoor or outdoor grid 20 yards long. The width of the grid is variable depending on the size of the squad.

Description
The player is to cover the length of the grid in a skipping motion. The knee moves from the centre of the body to a position outside the body line before returning to the central position. Return to the start by repeating the drill backwards.

Key teaching points
- Feet start in a linear position and move outwards as the knee is raised
- Work off the balls of the feet
- The knee is to be pushed, not rolled, out and back
- Maintain correct arm mechanics (*see* page 35)
- The movement should be smooth, not jerky

Sets and reps
2 × 20 yards, 1 forwards and 1 backwards.

Variations/progressions
Perform the drill laterally.

DRILL WIDE SKIP

Aim
To improve hip and ankle mobility, balance, co-ordination and rhythm. To increase body temperature.

Area/equipment
An indoor or outdoor grid 20 yards long. The width of the grid is variable depending on the size of the squad.

Description
The player is to cover the length of the grid by skipping, keeping the feet shoulder-width apart and the knees facing outwards at all times. Return to the start by repeating the drill backwards.

Key teaching points
- Keep off the heels
- Maintain correct arm mechanics (*see* page 35)
- Maintain an upright posture
- Do not take the thighs above 90°

Sets and reps
2 × 20 yards, 1 forwards and 1 backwards.

Variations/progressions
Perform the drill laterally.

DRILL *SINGLE-LEG HIGH-KNEE SKIP*

Aim
To improve buttock flexibility and hip mobility. To increase the ROM over a period of time. To develop rhythm. To increase body temperature.

Area/equipment
An indoor or outdoor grid 20 yards long. The width of the grid is variable depending on the size of the squad.

Description
The player is to cover the length of the grid using a high skipping motion with one leg only, and return to the start by repeating the drill in a backward motion. Repeat, using the other leg.

Key teaching points
- Thigh to be taken past 90°
- Work off the balls of the feet
- Maintain a strong core
- Maintain an upright posture
- Control the head by looking forwards at all times
- Maintain correct arm mechanics (*see* page 35)

Sets and reps
2 × 2 × 20 yards, 1 forwards and 1 backwards, first on the right leg and then on the left.

Variations/progressions
Perform the drill laterally.

DRILL   KNEE TO CHEST

Aim
To stretch the gluteals and improve linear hip mobility. To increase body temperature.

Area/equipment
An indoor or outdoor grid 20 yards long. The width of the grid is variable depending on the size of the squad.

Description
The player is to stand tall and to raise the knee of one leg up to the chest, lightly increase the stretch, and squeeze the knee in by placing the hands around the front of the knee and applying pressure. The foot is then returned to the ground and the drill repeated on the other leg.

Key teaching points
- Work off the ball of the foot on the straight leg
- Apply pressure steadily
- Stay tall and look ahead

Sets and reps
2×20 yards, 1 forwards and 1 backwards.

Variations/progressions
On releasing the leg use a knee-out step.

DRILL LATERAL RUNNING

Aim
To develop economic knee drive, stretch the side of the quadriceps and prepare for an efficient lateral running technique. To increase body temperature.

Area/equipment
An indoor or outdoor grid 20 yards long. The width of the grid is variable depending on the size of the squad.

Description
The player is to cover the length of the grid, leading with the left or right shoulder, and taking short lateral steps. Return leading with the opposite shoulder.

Key teaching points
- Keep the hips square
- Work off the balls of the feet
- Do not skip
- Do not let the feet cross over
- Maintain an upright posture
- Do not sink into the hips or lean over
- Do not overstride – use short, sharp steps
- Maintain correct arm mechanics (*see* page 35)

Sets and reps
2 × 20 yards, 1 with the left shoulder leading and 1 with the right.

Variations/progressions
Practice lateral, angled zigzag runs.

DRILL | CARIOCA

Aim

To improve hip mobility and speed, which will increase the firing rate of nerve impulses over time. To develop balance and co-ordination whilst moving and twisting. To increase body temperature.

Area/equipment

An indoor or outdoor grid 20 yards long. The width of the grid is variable depending on the size of the squad.

Description

The player is to cover the length of the grid by moving laterally. The rear foot crosses in front of the body and then moves around to the back. Simultaneously, the lead foot will do the opposite. The arms also move across the front and back of the body.

Key teaching points

- Start slowly and build up the tempo
- Work off the balls of the feet
- Keep the shoulders square
- Do not force the ROM
- Use the arms primarily for balance

Sets and reps

2 × 20 yards, 1 leading with the left leg and 1 with the right.

Variations/progressions

Perform the drill laterally with a partner (mirror drill) i.e. one leads the movement while the other attempts to follow.

DRILL   *PRE-TURN*

Aim
To prepare the hips for a turning action without committing the whole body. To increase body temperature and improve body control.

Area/equipment
An indoor or outdoor grid 20 yards long. The width of the grid is variable depending on the size of the squad.

Description
The player is to cover the length of the grid by performing a lateral movement. The heel of the back foot is moved to a position almost alongside the lead foot. Just before the feet come together, the lead foot is moved away laterally. Return to the start in the same way but lead with the opposite shoulder.

Key teaching points
- The back foot must not cross the lead foot
- Work off the balls of the feet
- Maintain correct arm mechanics (*see* page 35)
- Maintain an upright posture
- Do not sink into the hips or fold at the waist
- Do not use a high knee-lift – the angle should be no more than 45°

Sets and reps
2 × 20 yards, 1 leading with the left shoulder and 1 with the right.

DRILL | *SIDE LUNGE*

Aim
To stretch inner thighs and gluteals. To develop balance and co-ordination. To increase body temperature.

Area/equipment
An indoor or outdoor grid 20 yards long. The width of the grid is variable depending on the size of the squad.

Description
The player is to cover the length of the grid by performing lateral lunges. Take a wide lateral step and simultaneously lower the gluteals towards the ground. Return to the start leading with the opposite shoulder.

Key teaching points
- Do not bend at the waist or lean forward
- Try to keep off the heels
- Maintain a strong core and keep upright
- Use the arms primarily for balance

Sets and reps
2 × 20 yards, 1 leading with the left shoulder and 1 with the right.

Variations/progressions
Work in pairs facing each other and chest-passing the ball.

DRILL   TWIST AGAIN

Aim
To improve rotational hip mobility and speed. To develop balance, foot control and co-ordination and increase body temperature.

Area/equipment
An indoor or outdoor grid 20 yards long. The width of the grid is variable depending on the size of the squad.

Description
The player is to stand tall with his or her feet together and jump forwards moving the feet to the left and then across the body to the right. The arms should be fired across the body for balance and speed.

Key teaching points
- Try to develop a rhythm
- Work off the balls of the feet
- Maintain an upright posture and look ahead
- Do not sink into the hips or bend over at the waist
- Imagine that you are actually stepping over a barrier

Sets and reps
2 × 20 yards, 1 forwards and 1 backwards.

Variations/progressions
Perform the drill sideways, changing from left to right shoulders.

DRILL HURDLE WALK

Aim

To stretch inner and outer thighs, and increase ROM. To develop balance and co-ordination and increase body temperature.

Area/equipment

An indoor or outdoor grid 20 yards long. The width of the grid is variable depending on the size of the squad.

Description

The player is to cover the length of the grid by walking in a straight line and alternating the lifting leg as if going over a high hurdle. Return to the start by repeating the drill backwards.

Key teaching points

- Try to keep the body square as the hips rotate
- Work off the balls of the feet
- Maintain an upright posture
- Do not sink into the hips or bend over at the waist
- Imagine that you are actually stepping over a barrier

Sets and reps

2 × 20 yards, 1 forwards and 1 backwards.

DRILL　*BUTT KICKS*

Aim
To stretch front and back of thighs and to improve hip mobility. To increase body temperature.

Area/equipment
An indoor or outdoor grid 20 yards long. The width of the grid is variable depending on the size of the squad.

Description
The player is to cover the length of the grid by moving forwards alternating leg flicks where the heel moves up towards the buttocks. Return to the start by repeating the drill backwards.

Key teaching points
- Start slowly and build up the tempo
- Work off the balls of the feet
- Maintain an upright posture
- Do not sink into the hips
- Try to develop a rhythm

Sets and reps
2 × 20 yards, 1 forwards and 1 backwards.

Variations/progressions
- Perform the drill laterally
- Perform the drill as above but flick the heel to the outside of the buttocks

DRILL ICE SKATING

Aim
To increase hip and ankle mobility, lateral foot control, balance and co-ordination. To increase body temperature.

Area/equipment
An indoor or outdoor grid 20 yards long. The width of the grid is variable depending on the size of the squad.

Description
The player is to lean slightly forward and swing the arms across the body while sidestepping from left to right like an ice skater.

Key teaching points
- Keep the head up
- Do not sink into the hips or lean over
- Try to land on the balls of the feet

Sets and reps
2 × 20 yards, 1 leading with the left shoulder and 1 with the right.

Variations/progressions
Alternate from short step to long step.

DRILL ZIGZAG RUNS

Aim
To develop the ability of players to change direction in an efficient, balanced and effective manner. To increase body temperature.

Area/equipment
An indoor or outdoor grid 20 yards long. The width of the grid is variable depending on the size of the squad.

Description
The player is to cover the length of the grid by making short, zigzag runs. Each stage of the run is over about 2–3 yards before making a sharp change of direction. Return to the start by repeating the drill backwards.

Key teaching points
- Work off the balls of the feet
- Maintain correct arm mechanics (*see* page 35)
- Maintain a good posture
- Focus on short steps particularly when changing direction
- Push off the outside foot to change direction – do not pull with the inside foot

Sets and reps
2 × 20 yards, 1 forwards and 1 backwards.

Variations/progressions
Perform the drill very close to another player to simulate the close contact that may occur in a game.

DRILL JOCKEYING

Aim
To simulate defensive and attacking close-quarter movement patterns. To increase body temperature.

Area/equipment
An indoor or outdoor grid 20 yards long. The width of the grid is variable depending on the size of the squad.

Description
Players are to stand facing each other and to cover the grid working both forwards and backwards. The player moving forwards (attacker) will show the left then the right shoulder alternately in a rhythmic motion. The player moving backwards (defender) covers the attacking player's movements by mirroring them.

Key teaching points
- Take short steps
- Do not cross the feet
- Maintain a strong core and an upright posture
- Do not sink into the hips
- Keep your eyes on the opponent at all times

Sets and reps
2 × 20 yards, 1 leading with the left leg and 1 with the right.

Variations/progressions
Introduce the ball to the attacking player who presses, transferring the ball from left hand to right to keep the defender on his or her toes.

DRILL *FORWARD LUNGE*

Aim
To stretch front of hips and thighs. To develop balance and co-ordination and increase body temperature.

Area/equipment
An indoor or outdoor grid 20 yards long. The width of the grid is variable depending on the size of the squad.

Description
The player is to cover the length of the grid by performing a walking lunge. The front leg should be bent 90° at the knee with the thigh horizontal. The back leg should also be bent at 90° but with the knee touching the ground and the thigh vertical. Return to the start by repeating the drill backwards.

Key teaching points
- Try to keep the hips square
- Maintain a strong core and keep upright
- Maintain good control
- Persevere with backward lunges – these are difficult to master

Sets and reps
2 × 20 yards, 1 forwards and 1 backwards.

Variations/progressions
- Perform the drill with hand weights
- Perform the drill while catching and passing a ball in the down position

DRILL 2 JUMPS AND 3 STEPS

Aim
To develop the co-ordination and good foot-to-ground contact required for explosive linear running. To increase body temperature.

Area/equipment
An indoor or outdoor grid 20 yards long. The width of the grid is variable depending on the size of the squad.

Description
The player is to cover the length of the grid by completing sequences of 2 low, two-footed jumps followed immediately by 3 fast, short explosive linear steps. The player should alternate the foot used to take the first step. Return to the start by repeating the drill backwards.

Key teaching points
- Work off the balls of the feet
- Reassert good, strong arm mechanics during the transition from jumps to steps
- Keep the jumps low
- Focus on using small steps

Sets and reps
2 × 20 yards, 1 forwards and 1 backwards.

Variations/progressions
Make the 3 steps lateral or angled.

DRILL   *FAST FEET*

Aim
To develop the ability to move the feet very quickly and develop positive foot-to-ground contact. To increase body temperature.

Area/equipment
An indoor or outdoor grid 20 yards long. The width of the grid is variable depending on the size of the squad.

Description
The player is to cover the length of the grid by alternating between 'firing' their feet as fast as possible over 3–5 yards and then relaxing into a slow jog for about 5 yards. Return to the start by repeating the drill backwards.

Key teaching points
- Work off the balls of the feet
- Use of strong, fast arm mechanics
- Fit in as many steps as possible over the fast-foot area
- Maintain a good strong posture

Sets and reps
2 × 20 yards, 1 forwards and 1 backwards.

Variations/progressions
Perform the drill laterally.

DRILL   SPRINT LEG

Aim
To improve buttock flexibility and hip mobility. To isolate the correct 'running cycle' motion for each leg.

Area/equipment
An indoor or outdoor grid 20 yards long. The width of the grid is variable depending on the size of the squad.

Description
The player is to cover the length of the grid by bringing the knee of one leg quickly up to 90°. The other leg should remain as straight as possible with a very short lift away from the ground throughout the movement. Ratio should be 1:4, i.e. 1 lift to every 4 steps. Work one leg on the way down the grid and the other on the return.

Key teaching points
- Do not walk take the knee above 90°
- Strike the floor with the ball of the foot
- Keep the foot in a linear position
- Maintain correct running mechanics (*see* page 35)

Sets and reps
2 × 20 yards, 1 forwards and 1 backwards.

Variations/progressions
Vary the lift ratio, e.g. 1:2.

DRILL RUSSIAN WALK

Aim
To stretch the backs of the thigh and improve hip mobility and ankle stabilisation. To develop balance and co-ordination and increase body temperature.

Area/equipment
An indoor or outdoor grid 20 yards long. The width of the grid is variable depending on the size of the squad.

Description
The player is to cover the length of the grid by performing a walking march with a high extended step. Imagine that the aim is to scrape the sole of your shoe down the front of a door. Return to the start by repeating the drill backwards.

Key teaching points
- Lift the knee before extending the leg
- Work off the balls of the feet
- Try to keep off the heels, particularly on the back foot
- Keep the hips square

Sets and reps
2 × 20 yards, both forwards.

Variations/progressions
Perform the drill backwards.

DRILL WALKING HAMSTRING

Aim
To stretch the backs of the thighs.

Area/equipment
An indoor or outdoor grid 20 yards long. The width of the grid is variable depending on the size of the squad.

Description
The player is to cover the length of the grid by extending the lead leg heel-first on to the ground and rolling on to the ball of the foot. Walk forwards and repeat on the opposite leg, continue in this manner alternating the lead leg.

Key teaching points
- Keep the spine in a straight line
- Do not bend over
- Control the head by looking forward at all times
- Work at a steady pace, do not rush

Sets and reps
2 × 20 yards, 1 forwards and 1 backwards.

DRILL   *WALL DRILLS – LEG ACROSS BODY*

Aim
To increase the ROM in the hip region. To increase body temperature.

Area/equipment
A wall or fence to lean against.

Description
The player faces and leans against the wall or fence at an angle of about 20–30°. Swing the leg across the body from one side to the other. Repeat on the other leg.

Key teaching points
- Do not force an increased ROM
- Work off the ball of the support foot
- Lean with both hands against the wall or fence
- Keep the hips square
- Do not look down
- Gradually increase the speed

Sets and reps
7–10 on each leg.

Variations/progressions
Lean against a partner.

DRILL WALL DRILL – FORWARD LEG SWING

Aim
To increase the ROM in the hip region. To increase body temperature.

Area/equipment
A wall or fence to lean against.

Description
The player faces and leans against the wall or fence at an angle of about 20–30°. Take the leg back and swing it straight forward. Repeat with the other leg.

Key teaching points
- Do not force an increased ROM
- Work off the ball of the support foot
- Lean against the wall or fence
- Do not look down
- Gradually increase the speed

Sets and reps
7–10 on each leg.

Variations/progressions
Lean against a partner.

DRILL   *WALL DRILL – KNEE ACROSS BODY*

Aim
To increase the ROM in the hip region. To increase body temperature.

Area/equipment
A wall or fence to lean against.

Description
The player faces and leans against the wall or fence at an angle of about 20–30°. From a standing position, drive one knee upwards and across the body. Repeat on the other leg.

Key teaching points
- Do not force an increased ROM
- Work off the ball of the support foot
- Lean with both hands against the wall or fence
- Keep the hips square
- Do not look down
- Gradually increase the speed
- Imagine you are trying to get your knee up and across the body to the opposite pocket

Sets and reps
7–10 on each leg.

Variations/progressions
Lean against a partner.

DRILL SPRINTS

Aim
To increase the intensity of the warm-up and prepare players for maximum exertion. To speed up the firing rate of neuro-muscular messages. To increase body temperature.

Area/equipment
An indoor or outdoor grid 20 yards long. The width of the grid is variable depending on the size of the squad. Sprint one way only, performing a jog-back recovery on the outside of the grid.

Description
Players to start from different angles, e.g. side-on, backwards, etc. and to accelerate into a forward run down the grid.

Key teaching points
■ Maintain good running mechanics (*see* page 35)
■ Alternate the lead foot

Sets and reps
1 set of 5 sprints, varying the start position.

Variations/progressions
■ Include swerving sprints
■ Include turns in the sprints

DRILL   GRID VARIATIONS

Aim
To stimulate and motivate players with a variety of movement patterns.

Area/equipment
Mark out an indoor or outdoor grid 20 yards long with cones placed at 5-yard intervals. The width of the grid is variable depending on the size of the squad. Place a line of cones about 2 yards away from each side of the grid at approx. 2 yards away from the grid with 1 yard between each cone.

Description
Perform Dynamic Flex down the grid with the group splitting around the end cones to return on the outside of the grid. On reaching the cones the players should zigzag back through these.

Key teaching points
■ The timing is critical – players should be constantly on the move.

Sets and reps
Players can perform the entire Dynamic Flex warm-up in this manner.

Variations/progressions
Replace the cones on the outside of the grid with fast-foot ladders or hurdles.

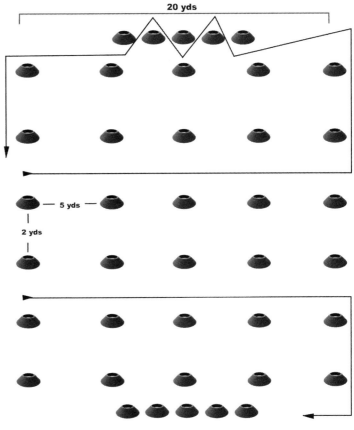

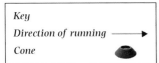

Figure 1.2 Grid variation

DRILL SPLIT GRID

Aim
To improve hockey-specific ball control and passing work.

Area/equipment
Mark out an indoor or outdoor grid 20 yards long with an additional 10 yards on the end (use different-coloured cones). The width of the grid is variable depending on the size of the squad.

Description
The player is to perform Dynamic Flex down the grid over the first 20 yards; on reaching the additional 10-yard area he or she picks the ball up and performs a hockey skill over the area and back. The next player should time the drill to collect the ball from the first, and so on.

Key teaching points
▨ Timing is critical – players should be constantly on the move.
▨ Players should communicate with one another
▨ The ball should not roll forwards – good hockey techniques are to be used
▨ Keep a straight spine – bend at the knees
▨ Try to keep the head up

Sets and reps
Players can perform the entire Dynamic Flex warm-up in this manner.

Variations/progressions
Vary the ball skill drills.

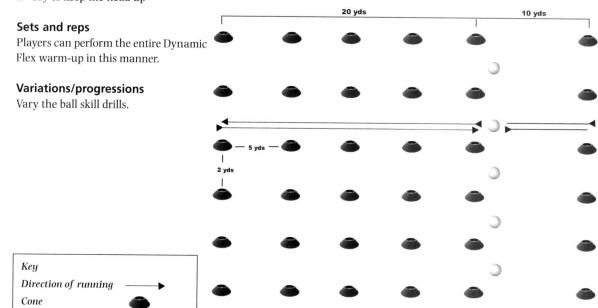

Key
Direction of running ⟶
Cone
Hockey ball

Fig 1.3 Split grid

COMBINATION WARM-UP GRIDS

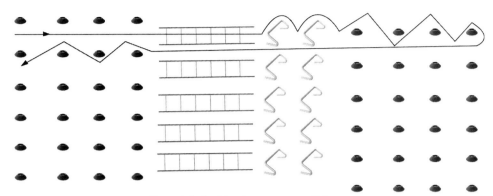

Figure 1.4 Combination warm-up grid 1

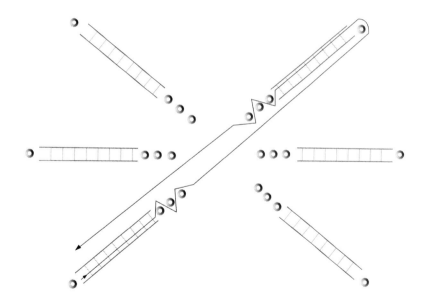

Figure 1.5 Combination warm-up grid 2 – multi-crossover

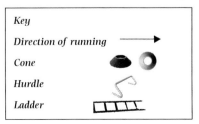

Key

Direction of running

Cone

Hurdle

Ladder

DYNAMIC FLEX CIRCLE GRID

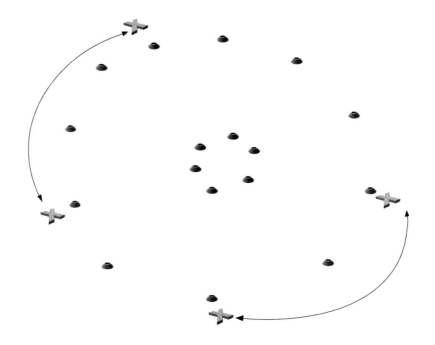

Figure 1.6 Dynamic Flex circle grid

MECHANICS OF MOVEMENT

Arm mechanics

With regard to running form and, in particular, arm mechanics, hockey players have an additional difficulty to overcome. The fact that they have to carry a hockey stick – usually in their right hand, less often in their left and frequently in both – makes for complications. If a player is covering a longer distance without the ball – perhaps when trying to support an attacking move – running in a more upright position with the stick in the right hand only is the most efficient way.

A player on the ball may occasionally have the space and the ability to dribble it using only one hand on the stick, and therefore adopt the more preferable upright running posture as well as having a free arm to aid balance and speed and to fend off the opposition! However, players will also be involved in close areas of play where tight ball-control is crucial; in these situations players will need to carry the stick in both hands – which will impact on their running form.

Players must be encouraged to recognise these different situations and trained to carry the stick and assert good arm mechanics as appropriate:

■ Elbows should be held at 90°

■ Hands should be relaxed

■ The insides of the wrists should brush against the pockets

■ The hands should move from the buttock cheeks to the chest

■ Reassert the arm drive as soon as possible after passing the ball or coming up from a lowered body position

Lift Mechanics

Hockey is a multi-sprint, stop/start sport, so the first phase of acceleration and re-acceleration are crucial. Over the years many players have been coached to run with a high knee action, probably due to a transfer from athletics sprint training. In actual fact, lifting the knees high, particularly in the first few yards of the acceleration phase, only makes one slower, and has the negative effect of minimizing force development, therefore not enough power is produced to propel the body forward in an explosive action. During this phase short, sharp steps are required, to generate a high degree of force that takes the body from a stationary position into the first controlled explosive steps.

It is important that players are encouraged to shorten stride length and increase the stride frequency when an approaching an opponent or making a sharp change in direction, thus maximising foot-to-ground contact. This allows the player to be in control of their power and direction enabling them to turn, twist, sidestep and reaccelerate through the gaps created. If a player maintains a long stride and their stride frequency is lower, there will be less foot-to-ground contact. Therefore a player contacted by an opponent is likely to be knocked off balance or slowed in changing direction.

Look and listen for:

■ Initial acceleration strides, knee lift of 45°

■ Floor contact with the ball of the foot

■ Front of the foot in a linear position

■ Knees coming up in a vertical line

■ Foot-to-floor contact should make a tapping noise, not a thud or a slap

- If the foot or the knee splay in or out, power will not be transferred correctly
- Keep off the heels
- On the lift, the foot will transfer from pointing slightly down to pointing slightly up

Posture

Posture is also an important part of acceleration and sprinting. The spine should be kept straight as much as possible at all times. A player who has tackled, dribbled and passed the ball and is running into space to support, needs to transfer to the correct running form as quickly as possible. Running with a straight spine does not mean running bolt upright; you can keep your spine straight when leaning slightly forward. What is to be avoided is players sinking into their hips – appearing to be folded up in the middle – because this prevents effective transfer of power.

Body Position

Hockey demands that the body position is lowered particularly in close-on-the-ball situations, when tackling and when the goalkeeper is involved. It is impossible for the human body to accelerate when in a lowered or bent position. Insisting that players run and stay low, will in fact make them slower and less powerful. What must be practised is regaining a posture of being as tall as possible, as quickly as possible after lowering the body to perform a task. Looking up and firing the arms helps with this process.

Mechanics for Deceleration

The ability of hockey players to stop quickly, change direction and accelerate away is a key area in building successful teams. This can be practised: do not leave it to chance, include it in your sessions.

- *Posture* – lean back: this alters the angle of the spine and hips which control foot placement. Foot contact with the ground will now transfer to the heel, which acts like a brake
- *Fire the arms* – by firing the arms quickly the energy produced will increase the frequency of heel contacts to the ground. Think of it like pressing harder on the brakes in a car

The running techniques described in this chapter cover basic mechanics for hockey-specific techniques where running, pushing, jumping and turning are all important parts of the game. These are developed through the use of hurdles, stride frequency canes and the practice of correct running form.

DRILL | ARM MECHANICS – PARTNER

Aim
To perfect the correct arm technique for running in hockey.

Area/equipment
The player works with a partner.

Description
The player stands with the partner behind. The partner holds the palms of his or her hands in line with the player's elbows, fingers pointing upwards. The player fires the arms as if sprinting so that the elbows smack into the partner's palms.

Key teaching points
- Arms should not move across the body
- Keep the elbows at 90°
- Hands and shoulders should be relaxed
- The insides of the wrists should brush against the pockets
- ROM – hands should move from buttock cheeks to chest or head
- Speed is important – the smack should be heard

Sets and reps
3 sets of 16 reps with 1 minute recovery between each set.

Variations/progressions
Use hand weights for the first 2 sets, perform the last set without.

DRILL ARM MECHANICS – MIRROR

Aim

To perfect the correct arm technique for running in hockey.

Area/equipment

A large mirror.

Description

The player stands in front of the mirror with arms ready for sprinting and performs short bursts of arm drives. Use the mirror as a feedback tool to perfect the technique.

Key teaching points

- Arms should not move across the body
- Keep elbows at 90°
- Keep hands and shoulders relaxed
- The insides of the wrists should brush against the pockets
- ROM – hands should move from the buttock cheeks to chest or head
- The player should perform a full ROM

Sets and reps

3 sets of 16 reps with 1 minute recovery between each set.

Variations/progressions

- Use hand weights for the first 2 sets, perform the last set without
- Introduce the stick and practise good arm mechanics

DRILL ARM MECHANICS – BUTTOCK BOUNCES

Aim
To develop explosive arm drive.

Area/equipment
Suitable ground surface.

Description
The player sits on the floor with legs straight out in front; the arms should be fired rapidly in short bursts. The power generated should be great enough to raise the buttocks off the floor in a bouncing action.

Key teaching points
- Arms should not move across the body
- Keep elbows at 90°
- Keep hands and shoulders relaxed
- The inside of the wrists should brush against the pockets
- ROM – hands should move from buttock cheeks to chest or head

Sets and reps
3 sets of 20 reps with 1 minute recovery between each set.

Variations/progressions
Use hand weights for the first 2 sets, perform the last set without.

DRILL   RUNNING FORM – DEAD-LEG RUN

Aim

To develop a quick knee-lift and the positive foot placement required for effective sprinting.

Area/equipment

Indoor or outdoor area. Using hurdles, cones or sticks, place about 8 obstacles in a straight line at 2-foot intervals. Place a cone 1 yard from each end of the line to mark a start and finish.

Description

The player must keep the outside leg straight in a locked position. The inside leg moves over the obstacles in a cycling motion while the outside leg swings along just above the ground (*see* fig. 2.1).

Key teaching points

- Bring the knee of the inside leg up to just below 90°
- Point the toe upwards
- Bring the inside leg back down quickly between the hurdles
- Increase the speed when the technique has been mastered
- Maintain correct arm mechanics
- Maintain an upright posture
- Keep the hips square and stand tall

Sets and reps

1 set of 6 reps, 3 with the left leg leading and 3 with the right.

Variations/progressions

- Use hand weights – accelerate off the end of the last obstacle and drop the hand weights during this phase
- Carry the stick throughout the drill

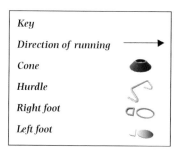

Figure 2.1 Dead-leg run

Key		
Direction of running	⟶	
Cone		
Hurdle		
Right foot		
Left foot		

DRILL   RUNNING FORM – LEADING LEG RUN

Aim
To develop quick, efficient steps and running technique.

Area/equipment
Indoor or outdoor area. Using hurdles, cones or sticks, place about 8 obstacles in a straight line at 2-foot intervals. Place a cone 1 yard from each end of the line to mark a start and finish.

Description
The player runs down the line of obstacles crossing over each one with the same lead leg. The player should aim to just clear the obstacles (*see* fig. 2.2). Repeat, leading with the other leg.

Key teaching points
- Knee drive should be no more than 45°
- Use short, sharp steps
- Maintain strong arm mechanics
- Maintain an upright posture
- Stand tall and do not sink into the hips

Sets and reps
1 set of 6 reps, 3 leading with the left leg and 3 with the right.

Variations/progressions
- Place 3 cones at the end of the obstacles at different angles about 2–3 yards away. On leaving the last obstacle, the player sprints out to the cone nominated by the coach. (This is good for developing the ability to change direction after running in a straight line.)
- Players carry their sticks and put them to the ground as though receiving a ball when they reach the nominated cone.
- Replace the cones with hockey balls so that players accelerate on to the ball.

Figure 2.2 Left- and right-leg lead

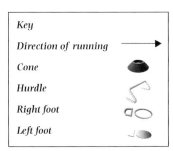

Key	
Direction of running	→
Cone	
Hurdle	
Right foot	
Left foot	

DRILL RUNNING FORM – LATERAL STEPPING

Aim
To develop efficient and economical lateral steps.

Area/equipment
Indoor or outdoor area. Using hurdles, cones or sticks, place about 8 obstacles in a straight line at 2-foot intervals. Place a cone 1 yard from each end of the line to mark a start and finish.

Description
The player steps over each obstacle while moving sideways (*see* fig. 2.3).

Key teaching points
- Bring the knee up to just below 45°
- Do not skip sideways – step!
- Push off from the back foot, do not pull with the lead foot
- Maintain correct arm mechanics
- Maintain an upright posture
- Keep the hips square
- Do not sink into the hips

Sets and reps
1 set of 6 reps, 3 leading with the left shoulder and 3 leading with the right.

Variations/progressions
- Use hand weights – accelerate off the end of the last obstacle and drop the hand weights during this phase
- Replace the cones with hockey balls so that players accelerate on to the ball
- Place a number of cones at various angles about 2–3 yards from the last hurdle. The player leaves the final hurdle and accelerates to the cone nominated by the coach

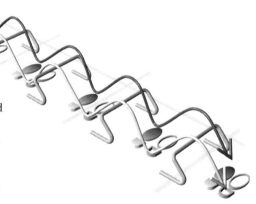

Figure 2.3 Lateral stepping

Key	
Direction of running	⟶
Cone	●
Hurdle	⌂
Right foot	⊂○
Left foot	⌐○

DRILL   *RUNNING FORM – PRE-TURN*

Aim
To educate and prepare the hips, legs and feet for effective and quick turning without fully committing the whole body.

Area/equipment
Indoor or outdoor area. Using hurdles, cones or sticks, place about 8 obstacles in a straight line at 2-foot intervals. Place a cone 1 yard from each end of the line to mark a start and finish.

Description
The player moves sideways along the line of obstacles just in front of them (not over them). The trailing leg is brought over the hurdle to a position slightly in front of the body so that the heel is in line with the toe of the leading foot. As the trailing foot is planted, the leading foot moves away (*see* fig. 2.4). Repeat the drill leading with the other leg.

Key teaching points
- Stand tall, do not sink into the hips
- Do not allow the feet to cross over
- Keep the feet shoulder-width apart as much as possible
- Knee-lift should be no greater than 45°
- Maintain correct arm mechanics
- Maintain an upright posture
- Keep the hips and shoulders square
- Work both the left and right sides

Sets and reps
1 set of 6 reps, 3 leading with the left shoulder and 3 with the right.

Variations/progressions
- Use hand weights – at the end of the obstacles, turn and accelerate 5 yards. Drop the weights halfway through this phase
- Replace the cones with hockey balls so that players accelerate on to the ball
- Place a number of cones at various angles about 2–3 yards from the last hurdle. The player leaves the final hurdle and turns to accelerate to the cone nominated by the coach.

Figure 2.4 Pre-turn

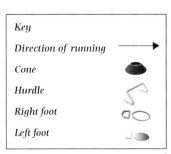

Key	
Direction of running	→
Cone	
Hurdle	
Right foot	
Left foot	

DRILL RUNNING FORM – CHANGING DIRECTION

Aim
To develop a player's ability to change direction with controlled precision and speed.

Area/equipment
Indoor or outdoor area. Using hurdles, cones or sticks, place 6–8 obstacles in an off-set zigzag formation (see fig. 2.5).

Description
The player moves forwards and laterally between the obstacles, and, on approaching each obstacle, steps over it with the outside foot only. As the foot contacts the ground, the player pushes off from it to change direction and approach the next obstacle.

Key teaching points
- Work off the balls of the feet
- Push off the outside foot when changing direction
- Do not pull with the inside foot
- Keep the hips square
- Maintain correct arm mechanics
- Ensure that short steps are used, particularly in the change of direction phase

Sets and reps
1 set of 6 reps.

Variations/progressions
- Players carry their sticks
- Vary the distances between the obstacles both linearly and laterally

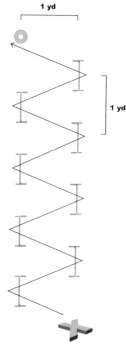

Key	
Direction of running	→
Cone	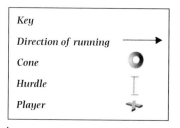
Hurdle	
Player	

Figure 2.5 Changing direction

DRILL   RUNNING FORM – 1–2–3 LIFT

Aim
To develop an efficient leg cycle, rhythm, power and foot placement.

Area/equipment
Indoor or outdoor area 30–40 yards long.

Description
The player moves in a straight line and after every third step the leg is brought up in an explosive action to 90° (*see* fig. 2.6). Continue the drill over the 30–40-yard grid with the same leg and then repeat with the other leg.

Key teaching points
- Keep the hips square
- Work off the balls of the feet
- Try to develop and maintain a rhythm
- Keep eyes and head up and look ahead
- Maintain correct arm mechanics
- Maintain an upright posture
- Keep the hips square

Sets and reps
1 set of 6 reps, 3 leading with the left leg and 3 with the right.

Variations/progressions
- Alternate the lead leg during a repetition
- Vary the lift sequence, e.g. 1–2–3–4 lift, etc.
- Carry a hockey stick

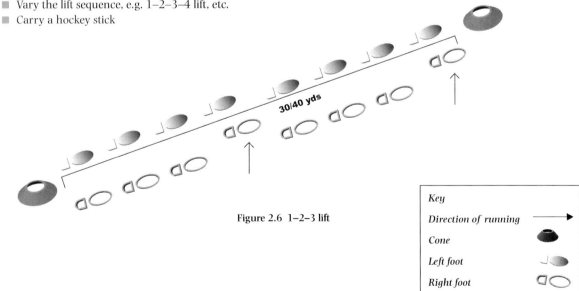

Figure 2.6 1–2–3 lift

Key	
Direction of running	→
Cone	●
Left foot	⌐◖
Right foot	⌐◯

DRILL JUMPING – TWO FOOTED SINGLE

Aim
To develop jumping techniques, power, speed and control.

Area/equipmen
Indoor or outdoor area. Ensure the surface is clear of any obstacles. Use 7-inch or 12-inch hurdles.

Description
The player jumps over a single hurdle and on landing walks back to the start point to repeat the drill (*see* fig. 2.7(a)).

Key teaching points
- Maintain good arm mechanics
- Do not sink into the hips at the take-off and landing phases
- Land on the balls of the feet
- Do not fall back onto the heels

Sets and reps
2 sets of 8 reps with 1 minute recovery between each set.

Variations/progressions
- Single jumps over the hurdle and back
- Single jump over the hurdle with a 180° twist (NB: practise twisting to both sides) (*see* fig. 2.7(b))
- Lateral single jumps – use both sides to jump off (*see* fig. 2.7(c))

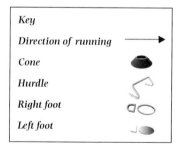

Key	
Direction of running	→
Cone	
Hurdle	
Right foot	
Left foot	

Figure 2.7(a) Two-footed single jump

Figure 2.7(b) Two-footed single jump with 180° twist

Figure 2.7(c) Two-footed lateral single jump

DRILL JUMPING – MULTIPLE JUMPS

Aim
To develop maximum control while taking off and landing. To develop controlled directional power.

Area/equipment
Indoor or outdoor area. Use 6–8 hurdles of 7 or 12 inches. Place these at 2-foot intervals in a straight line.

Description
The player jumps over each hurdle in quick succession until all have been cleared, walks back to the start and repeats the drill (*see* fig. 2.8(a)).

Key teaching points
- Use quick, rhythmic arm mechanics
- Do not sink into the hips on take-off and landing
- Land and take off from the balls of the feet
- Stand tall and look straight ahead
- Maintain control
- Gradually build up the speed

Sets and reps
2 sets of 6 reps with 1 minute recovery between each set.

Variations/progressions
- Lateral jumps (*see* fig. 2.8(b))
- Jumps with a 180° twist (*see* fig. 2.8(c))
- Hop over the hurdles, balance and then repeat (*see* fig. 2.8 (d))
- Use hand weights – do the last rep of each of these sets without the weights as a contrast

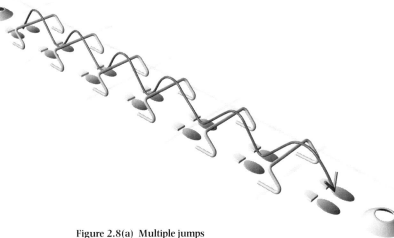

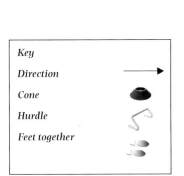

Key	
Direction	
Cone	
Hurdle	
Feet together	

Figure 2.8(a) Multiple jumps

47

JUMPING – MULTIPLE JUMPS

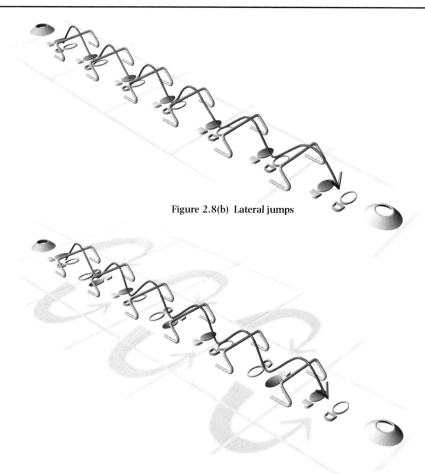

Figure 2.8(b) Lateral jumps

Figure 2.8(c) Lateral jumps with 180° twist

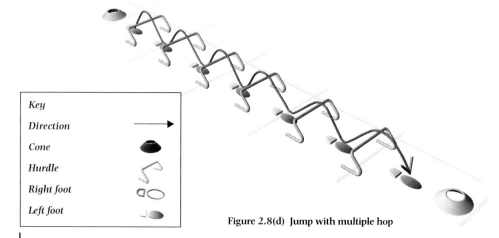

Key

Direction

Cone

Hurdle

Right foot

Left foot

Figure 2.8(d) Jump with multiple hop

RUNNING FORM –
DRILL   STRIDE FREQUENCY AND STRIDE LENGTH

Aim
To practise the transfer from the acceleration phase to an increase in stride frequency and length required when running. To develop an efficient leg cycle, rhythm, power and foot placement.

Area/equipment
Indoor or outdoor area 40–60 yards long. 12 coloured canes 4 feet in length are placed out on the ground at 5–6 foot intervals (the intervals will be determined by the size and age of the group).

Description
The player starts to accelerate 20 yards away from the first cane and aims to land just past each one. On leaving the last cane the player gradually decelerates, then returns to the start and repeats the drill (*see* fig. 2.9).

Key teaching points
- Do not overstride
- Work off the balls of the feet
- Try to develop and maintain a rhythm
- Keep eyes and head up as if looking over a fence
- Maintain correct mechanics
- Maintain an upright posture
- Stay focused

Sets and reps
1 set of 4 reps.

Variations/progressions
- Set up the stride frequency sticks as shown in fig. 2.9. The canes now control the acceleration and deceleration phases
- Add a change of direction during the deceleration phase
- Carry a stick throughout the drill
- Introduce a ball for players to dribble throughout the drill or that they pick up at a particular point on the grid
- Use hurdles rather than canes to encourage a higher knee-lift as appropriate

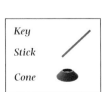

Key	
Stick	/
Cone	●

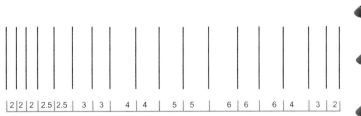

Figure 2.9 Stride length and frequency grid

DRILL RUNNING FORM – WITH STICK AND BALL

Aim
To maintain good mechanics when faced with hockey-specific stresses with the inclusion of a stick and ball. To improve decision-making ability.

Area/equipment
Indoor or outdoor area. Place 8 hurdles in a straight line, 2 feet apart. Place a cone at each end, about 2 yards from the first and last cones respectively.

Description
The coach stands at the end cone with a hockey ball. The player performs a mechanics drill through the hurdles and on clearing the final hurdle accelerates on to the ball that has been fed in at various angles by the coach (see fig. 2.10(a)).

Key teaching points
- Maintain correct mechanics
- Stay focused by looking ahead
- Fire the arms explosively when accelerating to the ball
- Carry the stick, in one hand only, for as long as is functionally possible

Sets and reps
3 sets of 6 reps. The sets should be made up of various mechanics drills.

Variations/progressions
- On clearing the final hurdle the player receives a pass from a player or coach on one side who then passes to another positioned on the other side (see fig. 2.10(b))
- On clearing the final hurdle the player receives a pass and performs a 360° turn before sprinting away (see fig. 2.10(c))
- On clearing the final hurdle the player receives a pass and performs a dodge before sprinting away

RUNNING FORM – WITH STICK AND BALL contd.

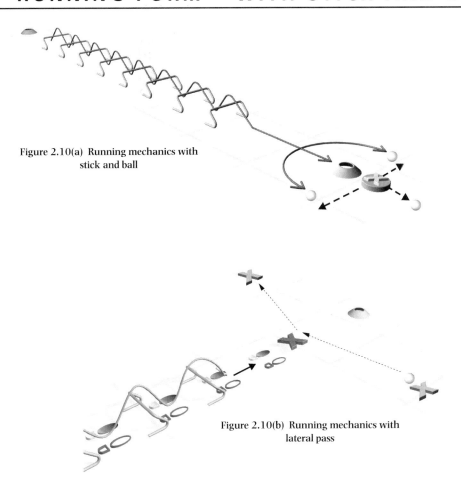

Figure 2.10(a) Running mechanics with stick and ball

Figure 2.10(b) Running mechanics with lateral pass

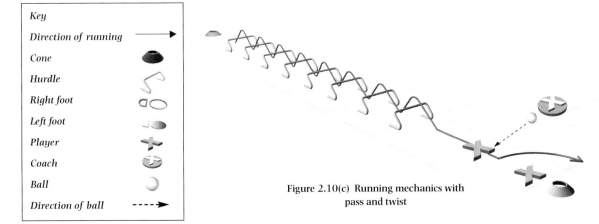

Key

Direction of running	→
Cone	
Hurdle	
Right foot	
Left foot	
Player	
Coach	
Ball	
Direction of ball	- - - →

Figure 2.10(c) Running mechanics with pass and twist

DRILL   RUNNING FORM – HURDLE MIRROR DRILLS

Aim
To improve the performance of mechanics under pressure and random agility.

Area/equipment
Indoor or outdoor area. Mark out a grid with 2 lines of 8 hurdles with 2 hurdle lengths between each hurdle and 2 yards between each line of hurdles.

Description
Players face each other while performing mechanics drills up and down the lines of hurdles. A player initiates the movements while a partner attempts to mirror them (*see* fig. 2.11(a)). Players can perform both lateral and linear mirror drills.

Key teaching points
- Stay focused on your partner
- The partner should try to anticipate the lead player's movements
- Maintain correct arm mechanics

Sets and reps
Each player performs 3 sets of 30-second work periods. Ensure 30 seconds recovery between each work period.

Variations/progressions
- First-to-the-ball drills – performed as above except a ball is placed between the two lines of hurdles. The proactive partner starts the drill as normal then accelerates to the ball, attempting to get there first and accelerate away with it. The reactive player tries to beat the proactive player to the ball (*see* fig. 2.11(b))
- Lateral drills performed as above – players work in pairs with only 3 hurdles per player (good for improving short-stepping lateral marking skills (*see* fig. 2.11(c))

RUNNING FORM – HURDLE MIRROR DRILLS contd.

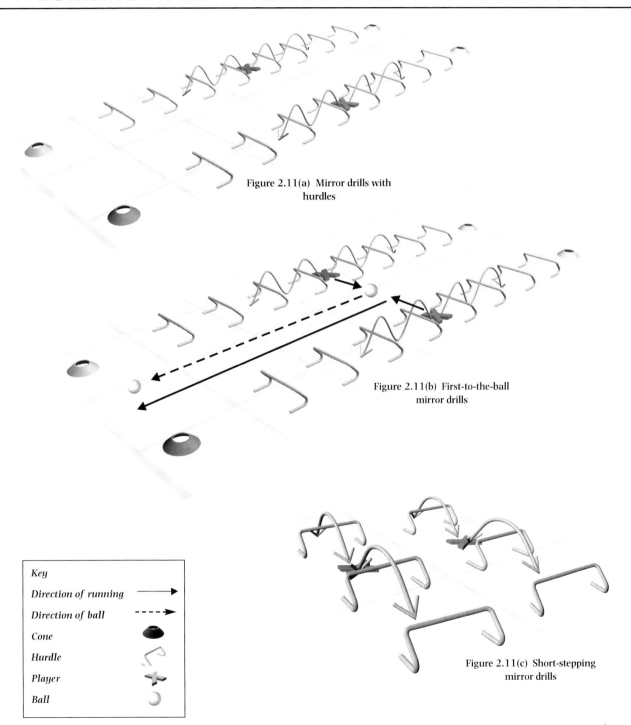

Figure 2.11(a) Mirror drills with hurdles

Figure 2.11(b) First-to-the-ball mirror drills

Figure 2.11(c) Short-stepping mirror drills

Key

Direction of running

Direction of ball

Cone

Hurdle

Player

Ball

DRILL RUNNING FORM – COMPLEX MECHANICS

Aim
To prevent players resorting to bad habits, particularly when under pressure. To challenge players by placing them under game-like pressure, and to maintain good running form even in the most difficult and demanding of situations.

Area/equipment
Indoor or outdoor area. Place 4 hurdles 2 feet apart in a straight line. The next 4 hurdles are set slightly to one side and the final 4 hurdles are placed back in line with the original 4 (*see* fig. 2.12(a)).

Description
The player performs a dead-leg run over the hurdles with the leg changing over the 4 centre hurdles, and returns to the start by repeating the process in the opposite direction.

Key teaching points
- Maintain correct arm mechanics
- Work off the balls of the feet
- Try to develop and maintain a rhythm
- Keep eyes and head up and look ahead
- Maintain correct arm mechanics
- Maintain an upright posture
- Keep the hips square

Sets and reps
4 sets of 4 reps.

Variations/progressions
Perform the drill laterally moving both forwards and backwards to cross the centre 4 hurdles (*see* fig. 2.12(b)).

RUNNING FORM – COMPLEX MECHANICS contd.

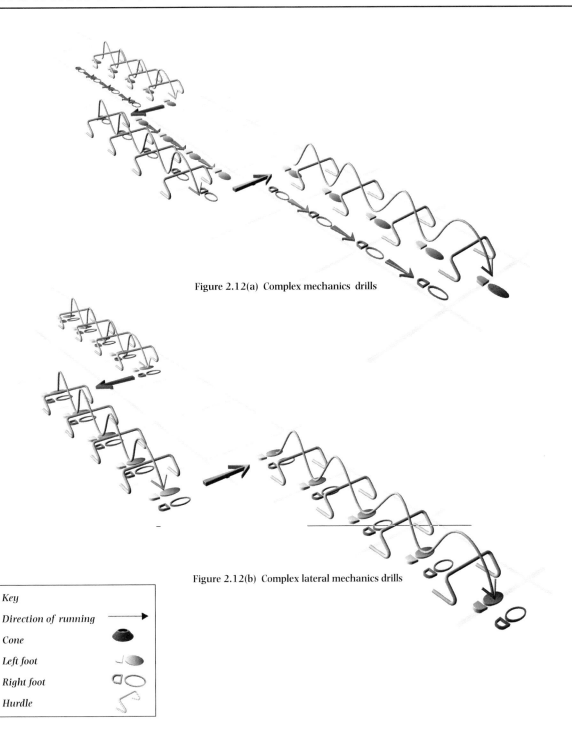

Figure 2.12(a) Complex mechanics drills

Figure 2.12(b) Complex lateral mechanics drills

Key

Direction of running

Cone

Left foot

Right foot

Hurdle

CHAPTER 3 INNERVATION

FAST FEET, AGILITY AND CONTROL FOR HOCKEY

This is the transition stage, from the warm-up and mechanics to periods of high-intensity work that activate the neural pathways. Using Fast Foot™ Ladders, dance-like patterns such as twists, jumps and turns are introduced, increasing the rate of firing in the neuro-muscular system, which acts as a strong motivator for players.

Once the basic footwork patterns have been mastered more advanced, hockey-specific footwork drills that require speed, co-ordination and agility can be introduced. The key here is to speed up the running techniques without compromising the quality of the mechanics. The innervation drills in this chapter progress from simple footwork patterns to complex hockey-specific drills that include ball and stick work.

DRILL FAST FOOT™ LADDER – SINGLE RUN

Aim
To develop fast feet with control, precision and power.

Area/equipment
Indoor or outdoor area. Use Fast Foot Ladder, ensuring that it is the correct one for the type of surface.

Description
The player moves the length of the ladder by placing one foot in each ladder space, and returns to the start by jogging or walking back beside the ladder (*see* fig. 3.1(a)).

Key teaching points
- Maintain correct running form/mechanics
- Start slowly and gradually increase the speed
- Maintain an upright posture
- Quality, not quantity, is important

Sets and reps
3 sets of 4 reps with 1 minute recovery between each set.

Variations/progressions
- Single lateral step – as above but performed laterally (*see* fig. 3.1(b))
- In-and-out – moving sideways along the ladder, stepping into and out of each space i.e. both feet in and both feet out (*see* fig. 3.1(c))
- Icky shuffle – sidestepping movement into and out of each space while moving forwards (*see* fig. 3.1(d))
- Double run – perform as single run but with both feet in each space (*see* fig. 3.1(e))
- Hopscotch (*see* fig. 3.1(f))
- Single-space jumps – two-footed jumps into and out of each space (*see* fig. 3.1(g))
- 2 squares forward and 1 square back (*see* fig. 3.1(h))
- Icky shuffle backwards

FAST FOOT™ LADDER – SINGLE RUN contd.

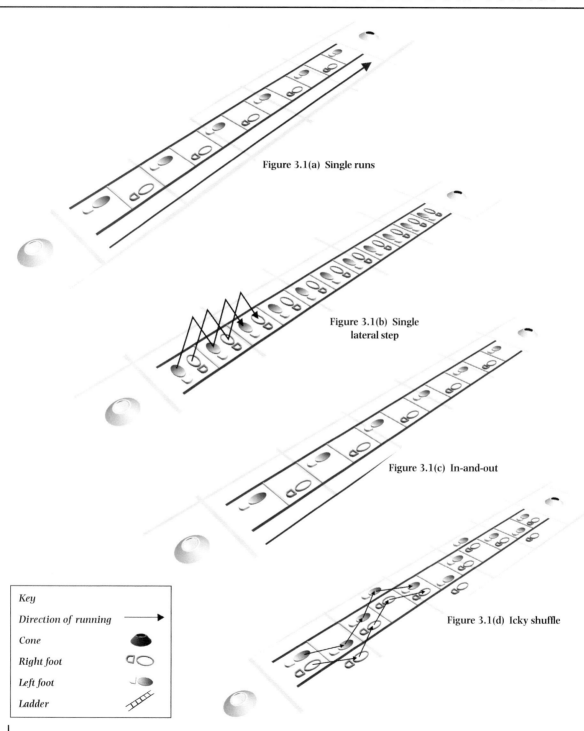

Figure 3.1(a) Single runs

Figure 3.1(b) Single
lateral step

Figure 3.1(c) In-and-out

Figure 3.1(d) Icky shuffle

Key

Direction of running

Cone

Right foot

Left foot

Ladder

FAST FOOT™ LADDER – SINGLE RUN contd.

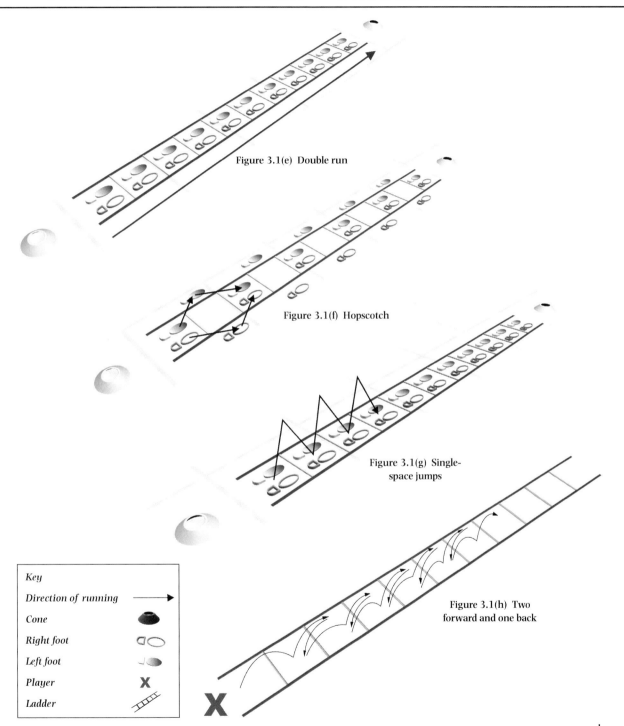

Figure 3.1(e) Double run

Figure 3.1(f) Hopscotch

Figure 3.1(g) Single-
space jumps

Figure 3.1(h) Two
forward and one back

Key

Direction of running

Cone

Right foot

Left foot

Player   X

Ladder

DRILL   FAST FOOT LADDER – T FORMATION

Aim

To develop speed and control of acceleration when pressing or attacking the opposition. To develop controlled lateral pressing skills and co-ordinated backward movement prior to turning and chasing.

Area/equipment

Indoor or outdoor area. Place 2 ladders in a T formation with 3 cones at the end of each ladder.

Description

The player accelerates down the ladder using single steps. On reaching the ladder and crossing the end, the player moves either left or right using short lateral steps. On coming out of the ladder the player then jockeys backwards keeping both the eyes and head forward.

Key teaching points

- Maintain correct running form/mechanics
- Use a strong arm drive when transferring from linear to lateral steps
- When moving backwards keep the head and eyes up
- Do not skip backwards
- Do not fall back onto the heels when moving backwards

Sets and reps

3 sets of 4 reps with 1 minute recovery between each set (2 to the left and 2 moving to the right)

Variations/progressions

- Players should carry their sticks
- Start with a lateral run and upon reaching the end ladder accelerate in a straight line forwards down the ladder
- Mix and match previous Fast Foot Ladder drills described earlier (*see* page 57)
- Up, across and drive – place a ball 2 yards away at both ends of the ladder for the player to accelerate on to

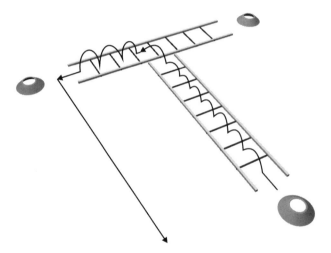

Figure 3.2 Up, across and jockey backwards

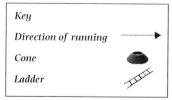

Key	
Direction of running	→
Cone	●
Ladder	▱▱▱

| DRILL | **FAST FOOT LADDER – CROSSOVER** |

Aim

To develop speed, agility and change of direction in a more hockey-specific crowded area. To improve reaction time, peripheral vision and timing.

Area/equipment

Large indoor or outdoor area. Place 4 ladders in a cross formation leaving a clear centre square of about 3 square yards. Place a cone 1 yard from the start of each ladder.

Description

Split the squad in to 4 equal groups and locate them at the start of each ladder (A, B, C and D). Simultaneously players accelerate down the ladder performing a single-step drill, then accelerate across the centre square and down the outside of the opposite ladder to join the end of the queue (*see* fig. 3.3(a)).

Key teaching points

- Maintain correct running form/mechanics
- Keep the head and eyes up and be aware of other players particularly around the centre area

Sets and reps

3 sets of 6 reps with 1 minute recovery between each set.

Variations/progressions

- Carry a hockey stick
- At the end of the first ladder cut to the right or left and join the appropriate adjacent ladder (*see* fig. 3.3(b))
- Vary the fast-foot drills performed down the first ladder
- Include a 360° turn in the centre square so that players spin off one another – this develops positional awareness
- Introduce hockey balls at the ends of the ladders to be dribbled or passed across the centre space

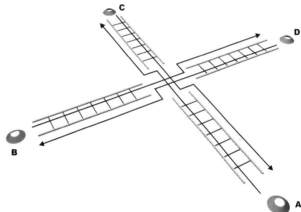

Figure 3.3(a) Crossover drill

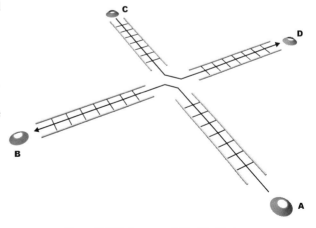

Figure 3.3(b) Crossover drill with sidestep

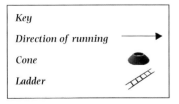

Key	
Direction of running	→
Cone	
Ladder	

DRILL   *FAST FOOT LADDER – WITH STICK AND BALL*

Aim
To develop fast feet, speed and agility while incorporating game-specific ball control.

Area/equipment
Large indoor or outdoor area. Place a Fast Foot Ladder with a cone about 1 yard from each end.

Description
While a player is performing lateral fast-foot drills down the ladder, a second player standing 2 yards away from the ladder in a central position feeds the ball into the player at different heights requiring the first player to step forwards, control and return the ball. (*See* fig. 3.4.)

Key teaching points
■ Concentrate on good footwork patterns
■ Use correct technical skills when controlling and returning the ball
■ The player performing the drill should return to correct running form/mechanics after returning the ball

Sets and reps
3 sets of 6 reps with 1 minute recovery between each set.

Variations/progressions
Goalkeepers to wear gloves and kickers and perform saves.

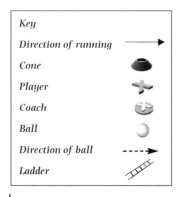

Key	
Direction of running	→
Cone	◗
Player	✛
Coach	⊕
Ball	○
Direction of ball	---→
Ladder	▱▱

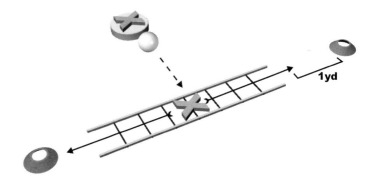

Figure 3.4 Fast Foot ladder drill with ball

DRILL　*FAST FOOT LADDER – PASSING*

Aim

To develop fast feet and agility while incorporating hockey-specific ball control and passing combination drills with good timing.

Area/equipment

Large indoor or outdoor area. Place 2–4 Fast Foot Ladders opposite each other with a 10–15-yard gap between them (*see* fig. 3.5(a)) and hockey balls at the end of each ladder.

Description

Divide into 2 or 4 groups depending on overall size. Players begin at the far end of each ladder and simultaneously perform the nominated fast-foot drill. On reaching the end of the ladder each player picks up the ball and accelerates across the middle space, leaving the ball at the end of the opposite ladder for the next player, before rejoining the queue.

Key teaching points

- Maintain correct running form/mechanics
- Use correct technical skills when on the ball
- Glance up as often as possible to ensure that collisions are avoided
- Try to time runs so that no one has to wait for the ball

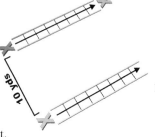

Figure 3.5(a) Fast Foot Ladders with passing drill

Sets and reps

3 sets of 6 reps with a 1 minute recovery between each set.

Variations/progressions

- Vary the ladder drill being performed
- Introduce a pass across the gap rather than dribbling the ball
- Vary the type of pass used
- Open up the middle space for a longer pass or run
- Players to dodge one another in the middle space
- Make the pass on a diagonal and maintain a straight run (*see* fig. 3.5(b))

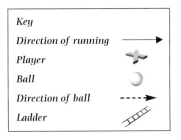

Key	
Direction of running	→
Player	
Ball	
Direction of ball	---→
Ladder	

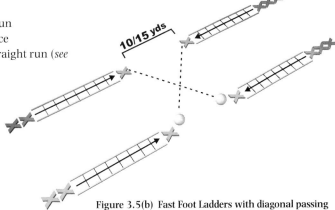

Figure 3.5(b) Fast Foot Ladders with diagonal passing

DRILL FAST FOOT LADDER – CLOSE CONTACT

Aim

To develop fast feet, agility and control in a restricted area while under pressure from other players.

Area/equipment

Large indoor or outdoor area. Place 4 ladders side by side.

Description

Work in pairs, one player on each of the outside ladders, and perform fast-foot drills down the length of the ladder. On the coach's signal the players will move to the centre ladders and work side by side (*see* fig. 3.6(a)).

Key teaching points

- Maintain correct running form/mechanics
- Players to push and nudge each other to simulate the close contact situations that occur in a game
- Players knocked off balance should reassert the correct arm mechanics as soon as possible

Sets and reps

3 sets of 4 reps with 1 minute recovery between each set.

Variations/progressions

- Players start from the centre ladders and work out and back in
- Players start on ladders next to each other on either the left or right of the grid and work across the 4 ladders (*see* fig. 3.6(b))
- Introduce sticks
- Competition – place a ball on the ground in the centre area, 2 yards away from the end of the ladders; the players compete to win the ball

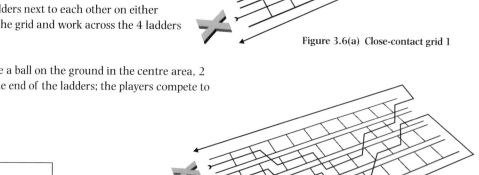

Figure 3.6(a) Close-contact grid 1

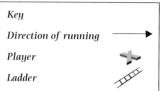

Key	
Direction of running	→
Player	⨯
Ladder	▱

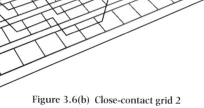

Figure 3.6(b) Close-contact grid 2

DRILL   *FAST FOOT LADDER – PASS SUPPORT*

Aim
To develop fast, controlled acceleration and the ability to pass and control the ball in a restricted area and to change direction to support the player on the ball.

Area/equipment
Large indoor or outdoor area of about 35 square yards; 7 ladders and balls. Place 3 ladders in a straight line next to one another, 5 yards apart. Off-set from these, and 10–20 yards from the end of the first line of ladders, place the other 4 next to each other other, 5 yards apart (*see* fig. 3.7). Two players or coaches stand at the extreme left and right between 2 sets of ladders.

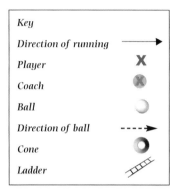

Description
Working in groups of 3 the players accelerate down the ladders in a slightly staggered formation, the player on the end ladder first, on the middle ladder second and on the third ladder last. A ball is fed in and passed from one side to the other by players coming off the ladder. On passing the ball each player steps in to support the ball before accelerating down the second ladder. (*See* fig. 3.7.)

Key teaching points
- Players should communicate well
- Maintain correct running form/mechanics
- Each player should carry the ball for a specified distance before passing it on
- Players must use the correct techniques when passing and dribbling the ball
- As soon as the ball is passed on players should reassert the correct arm mechanics

Sets and reps
3 sets of 5 reps with a walk-back recovery between each repetition and 2 minutes recovery between each set.

Variations/progressions
Introduce defenders or cones 3 yards away from the first 3 ladders; the player either beats the defender and passes the ball on or uses the pass to beat the defender then supports the player with the ball.

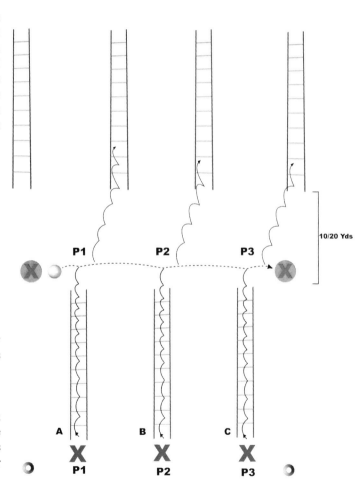

Figure 3.7 Supporting the pass

DRILL *LINE DRILLS*

Aim
To develop quickness of the feet.

Area/equipment
Indoor or outdoor area. Use any line marked on the ground.

Description
The player performs single split steps over the line and back (*see* fig. 3.8(a)).

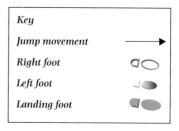

Key

Jump movement

Right foot

Left foot

Landing foot

Key teaching points
■ Maintain good arm mechanics
■ Maintain an upright posture
■ Maintain a strong core
■ Try to develop a rhythm
■ Keep the head and eyes up

Sets and reps
3 sets of 20 reps with 1 minute recovery between each set.

Variations/progressions
■ Two-footed jumps over the line and back (*see* fig. 3.8(b))
■ Stand astride the line and bring the feet in and onto the line before moving them back out again; perform the drill as quickly as possible (*see* fig. 3.8(c))
■ Two-footed side jumps over the line and back (*see* fig. 3.8(d))
■ Two-footed side jumps with a twist in the air over the line and back (*see* fig. 3.8(e))
■ Complex variation – introduce the ball either at the end of the drill to explode on to or during the drill to pass back

Always revert to good arm mechanics after passing the ball back

Figure 3.8(a) Single split steps

Figure 3.8(b) Two-footed jumps

Figure 3.8(c) Astride jumps

Figure 3.8(d) Two-footed side jumps over and back

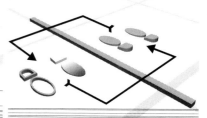

Figure 3.8(e) Two-footed side jumps with 180° twist

DRILL *QUICK BOX STEPS*

Aim
To develop explosive power and control, with the emphasis on speed.

Area/equipment
Indoor or outdoor area. Use a strong box, bench or aerobics step with a non-slip surface, about 12 inches high.

Description
The player performs split steps on the box, i.e. one foot on the box and one on the floor, alternating feet (*see* fig. 3.9(a)).

Key teaching points
- Focus on good arm drive
- Maintain an upright posture
- Maintain a strong core
- Keep the head and eyes up
- Work off the balls of the feet
- Work at high intensity
- Try to develop a rhythm

Sets and reps
3 sets of 20 reps with 1 minute recovery between each set.

Variations/progressions
- Two-footed jumps on and off of the box (*see* fig. 3.9(b))
- Two-footed side jumps on and off of the box (lead with the left shoulder for 10 reps then the right for 10 reps) (*see* fig. 3.9(c))
- Lateral split jumps (*see* fig. 3.9(d))
- Single-footed hops on and off the box (10 reps each foot) (*see* fig. 3.9(e))
- Double alternate single hop – single hop onto the box to land on the opposite foot. Take off to land on the other side of the box, again on the opposite foot (*see* fig. 3.9(f))

Key	
Jump movement	⟶
Right foot	⊂◯
Left foot	◖◗

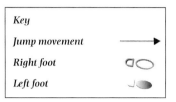

Figure 3.9(a) Alternating split step

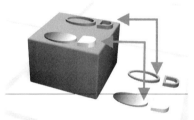

Figure 3.9(b) Two-footed jumps

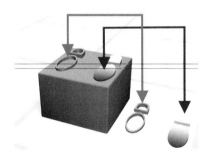

Figure 3.9(c) Two-footed side jumps

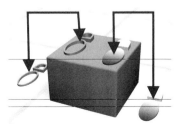

Figure 3.9(d) Straddle split-jumps

Figure 3.9(e) Single-footed hops

Figure 3.9(f) Double alternate single hop

CHAPTER 4 ACCUMULATION OF POTENTIAL

THE SAQ HOCKEY CIRCUIT

This is the part of the continuum which brings together those areas of work already practised. Many of the mechanics and fast-foot drills are specific to developing a particular skill. In hockey the skills are rarely isolated but occur in quick succession or in combinations. An example of this is when a player needs to run at full speed for 30 yards, decelerate, change direction and engage an opponent before peeling to pick up a ball and accelerate away. Combinations of manoeuvres, of course, occur over different time-spans.

Using ladders, hurdles, cones, poles etc., hockey-specific circuits can be used to develop programmed agility as well as to condition the player for this type of high-intensity work.

This phase should not fatigue the players. Ensure a maximum recovery period between sets and reps.

DRILL   *AGILITY RUNS – 4-SQUARE BALL*

Aim
To develop multi-directional explosive speed, turn and running mechanics both with and without the ball.

Area/equipment
Indoor or outdoor area of about 10 square yards. Place 5 cones, one on each corner and 1 in the middle. Place hockey balls in the centre around the cone.

Description
Carrying a stick, a player starts at the centre cone (E), grabs a ball and accelerates to cone (A), where the ball is placed on the cone. The player then returns to the centre cone and picks up another ball, accelerates to cone (B) and places the ball on the cone. The drill is completed when the final ball has been placed on cone (D) and the player has accelerated to finish at the centre cone. (*See* fig. 4.1.)

Key teaching points
- Maintain correct running form/mechanics
- Use strong arm mechanics when not dribbling the ball
- Do not allow the feet to cross over on the turn
- Resume efficient running form after placing the ball
- Use short steps and work off the balls of the feet at all times

Sets and reps
5 reps with 2 minutes recovery between each rep.

Variations/Progressions
- Players go round the corner cones
- Players use only 1 ball to effect a continuous dribbling drill

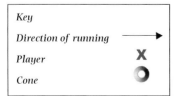

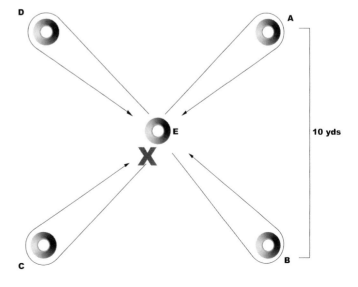

Figure 4.1 Agility run – 4-square ball

DRILL   AGILITY RUNS – T-RUN

Aim
To develop hockey-specific speed and agility.

Area/equipment
Indoor or outdoor area; 4 poles or cones. Place the poles or cones 5 yards apart in a T formation (*see* fig. 4.2(a)).

Description
Carrying a stick, a player starts on the left-hand side of the first pole, accelerates to the one directly ahead, passes it and turns right before accelerating to the end pole. The player then runs round the end pole and returns to the middle pole before finishing at the opposite side on the start position (*see* fig. 4.2(b)). Repeat the drill, starting on the right and reversing the direction of the turns.

Key teaching points
- Maintain correct running form/mechanics
- Work on shortening the steps used in the turn
- Focus on increasing the speed of the arm drive when coming out of the turns
- Work your weak side (most players will have a preferred turning side)

Sets and reps
3 sets of 5 reps with 30 seconds recovery between each rep and 1 minute recovery between each set.

Variations/progressions
- The coach stands at the centre cone. The player accelerates towards the coach who provides a verbal or visual signal to indicate which way to turn.
- Goalkeepers should wear their kit
- Perform the drill whilst dribbling a ball

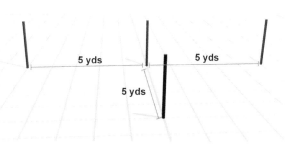

Figure 4.2(a) T-run grid

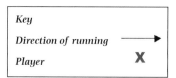

Key

Direction of running   ⟶

Player   **X**

Figure 4.2(b) T-run right

DRILL AGILITY RUNS – SWERVE DEVELOPMENT

Aim
To develop fine-angle running at pace and the ability to explode into a gap and create uncertainty in the opposition.

Area/equipment
A large indoor or outdoor area. Place 8–12 poles or cones in a zigzag formation (*see* fig. 4.3). The poles should be 2–4 yards apart at varying angles (to make the runs more realistic). The total length of the run will be 25–30 yards.

Description
Carrying a stick, the player accelerates from the first cone and swerves in and around all the cones before completing the course, then gently jogs or walks back to the starting cone before repeating the drill.

Key teaching points
- Maintain correct running form/mechanics
- Work on shortening the steps used in the turn
- Focus on increasing the speed of the arm drive when coming out of the turns
- Do not take wide angles around the cones
- Keep the head and eyes up

Sets and reps
3 sets of 5 reps with 30 seconds recovery between each rep and 1 minute recovery between each set.

Variations/progressions
- Use hand weights for the first 4 reps then perform the last rep without them as a contrast
- Perform the drill whilst dribbling a ball

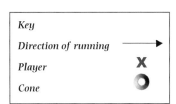

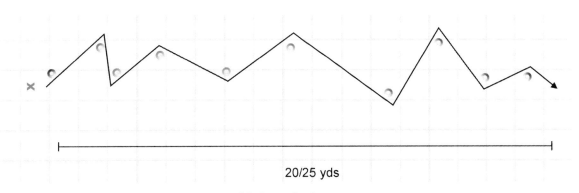

20/25 yds

Figure 4.3 Swerve-development runs

DRILL   AGILITY RUNS – ZIGZAG

Aim
To develop fast and controlled angled lateral runs.

Area/equipment
Indoor or outdoor area. Mark out a grid using 10–12 cones or poles in 2 staggered lines of 5–6 (*see* fig. 4.4(a)).

> Arm mechanics are as vital in lateral movements as they are in linear movements. Many players forget to use their arms when they are moving sideways.

Description
Carrying a stick the player runs along the zigzag staying on the inside of the cones then walking back to the start before repeating the drill.

Key teaching points
- Maintain correct running form/mechanics
- Keep hips facing the direction of running
- Use short steps
- Do not skip
- Use good arm mechanics

Sets and reps
3 sets of 6 reps with a walk-back recovery between each rep and 1 minute recovery between each set.

Variations/progressions
- Perform the drill backwards
- Go round each cone rather that staying on the inside
- Up and back – enter the grid sideways, move forwards to the first cone then backwards to the next, etc.
- Add a fast-foot ladder to the start and finish for acceleration and deceleration running (*see* fig. 4.4(b))
- Complete the above drills while dribbling a ball

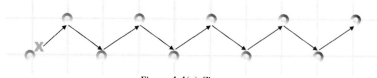

Figure 4.4(a) Zigzag run

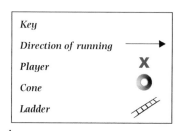

Key	
Direction of running	→
Player	**X**
Cone	◉
Ladder	⊞

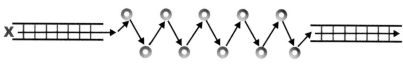

Figure 4.4(b) Ladder zigzag run

DRILL   AGILITY RUN – W DRILL

Aim
To develop multi-directional explosive speed and the ability to change direction quickly and efficiently.

Area/equipment
Indoor or outdoor area. Place 5 cones or poles in a W formation (*see* fig. 4.5(a)), place an additional 2 cones to mark the start and finish.

Description
Carrying a stick the player starts at cone 1 and accelerates forward to cone A. Facing forwards throughout the entire drill, the player goes from cone A to B and completes the W in this manner (*see* fig. 4.5(b)). Recover after cone 2, then repeat in the opposite direction.

Key teaching points
- Use strong arm mechanics
- Maintain correct running form/mechanics
- Focus on small steps particularly when changing direction
- Work off the balls of the feet

Sets and reps
3 sets of 6 reps (3 starting from cone 1 and 3 from cone 2) with 30 seconds recovery between each rep and 1 minute between sets.

Variations/progressions
- Perform the drill while dribbling a ball
- Players are to go around the cones
- Goalkeepers to complete the drill wearing their kit

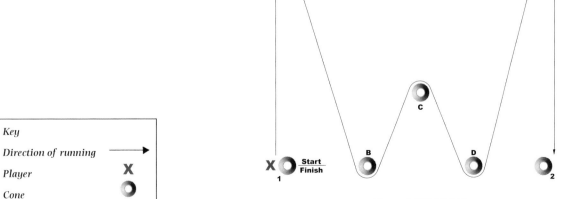

Figure 4.5(a) W formation

Figure 4.5(b) W drill

Key
Direction of running ———▶
Player   X
Cone   ◉

DRILL   HOCKEY-SPECIFIC CIRCUIT

Aim

To develop speed endurance through hockey-specific running patterns required in game situations.

Area/equipment

Half a hockey pitch or an equivalent size area – cones; hurdles, ladders and hockey balls to be placed in a circuit (*see* fig. 4.6).

Description

Carrying sticks, players will complete the circuit through ladders, over hurdles and around cones in a way that simulates the movements required in a game. Circuits should take 30–90 seconds depending on the phase in the season and the session focus.

Key teaching points

- Maintain correct running form/mechanics for all activities
- Ensure that correct techniques are used on the ball

Sets and reps

1 set of 6 reps with a varied recovery time between each rep depending on the stage in the season. Generally work on a work to rest ratio of 1:3 or 1:2.

Variations/progressions

- Vary the circuit to keep players motivated and challenged
- Introduce balls at various points in the circuit

HOCKEY-SPECIFIC CIRCUIT contd.

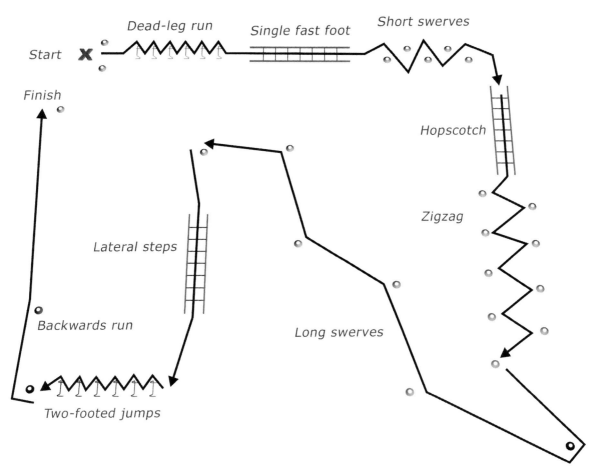

Figure 4.6 Hockey-specific runs

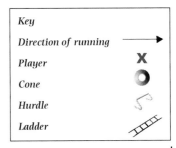

CHAPTER 5 EXPLOSION

3-STEP, MULTI-DIRECTIONAL ACCELERATION FOR HOCKEY

The exercises outlined in the chapter have been designed to boost response-times and develop multi-directional, explosive movements.

Programmable and random agility is trained using resisted and assisted high-quality plyometrics. Plyometric exercises focus on the stretch–shortening cycle of the muscles involved, an action that is a central part of hockey performance. Plyometric drills include drop-jumps, hops, skips and bounds. Plyometrics can be fun and challenging and adds variety to training sessions. However, there is potential for injury with these exercises so they must be performed using the correct technique and at the correct point in the training session.

Upper-body speed and power are also catered for with jelly-ball workouts, which are effective for the type of strength required to hold off an opponent.

The crucial element in using explosive drills is the implementation of the 'contrast' phase. This simply means performing the drill without resistance for one or two reps immediately after performing it with resistance. These movements will naturally be more explosive and more easily remembered and reproduced over a period of time. The key is to ensure that quality not quantity is the priority. Efforts must be carefully monitored.

> This is a time for high-intensity explosive action, not 'tongue-hanging out fatigue'!

DRILL SEATED FORWARD GET-UPS

Aim
To develop multi-directional explosive acceleration. To improve a player's ability to get up and accelerate all in one movement.

Area/equipment
Indoor or outdoor area of 20 square yards.

Description
The player sits on the floor with legs straight out in front. On the coach's signal the player gets up as quickly as possible, accelerates forward for 10 yards, then slows down before jogging gently back to the start.

Key teaching points
- Try to complete the drill in one smooth action
- Use correct running form/mechanics
- Do not stop between getting up and running
- Get into an upright position and drive the arms as soon as possible
- Initial steps must be short and powerful
- Do not overstride

Sets and reps
3 sets of 5 reps with a jog-back recovery between each rep and 2 minutes recovery between each set.

Variations/progressions
- Seated backward get-ups
- Seated sideways get-ups
- Lying down get-ups (front, back, left and right)
- Kneeling get-ups
- Work in pairs and have get-up competitions – first to the ball
- Work in pairs with one player in front of the other and perform tag get-ups
- Goalkeepers to wear kit

DRILL *FORWARD LET-GO*

Aim
To develop multi-directional explosive acceleration.

Area/equipment
Indoor or outdoor area of 20 square yards; Viper Belt with hand leash.

Description
Player 1 wears the Viper Belt and carries a stick; then attempts to accelerate away in a straight line forward while being resisted from behind by Player 2 who holds the hand leash to provide resistance. Player 2 maintains the resistance for a couple of seconds before releasing Player 1 who explodes away. (If a Viper Belt and hand leash are not available, hold on to the shirt/top of Player 1.)

Key teaching points
- Player 1 should not lean or pull forward excessively
- Use short steps during the explosion and acceleration phases
- Use good arm drive
- Player 1 should adopt good running form/mechanics as soon as possible

Sets and reps
3 sets of 5 reps with a walk-back recovery between each rep and 2 minutes recovery between each set.

Variations/progressions
- Lateral let-goes
- Backwards let-goes
- Let-goes with an acceleration onto a stationary ball
- Let-goes with an acceleration onto a moving ball
- Goalkeepers to wear kit

DRILL FLEXI-CORD – BUGGY RUNS

Aim
To develop multi-directional explosive acceleration.

Area/equipment
Indoor or outdoor area – ensure that there is plenty of room for safe deceleration. 1 Viper Belt with a Flexi-cord attached at both ends by 2 anchor points. Place 3 cones in a line, 10 yards apart.

Description
Work in pairs. Player 1 wears the belt while Player 2 stands behind holding the Flexi-cord, hands looped in and over the cord (for safety purposes). Player 2 allows resistance to develop as Player 1 accelerates forward, then runs behind maintaining constant resistance over the first 10 yards. Both players need to decelerate over the second 10 yards. Player 1 removes the belt after the required number of reps and completes a solo contrast run. Repeat the drill but swap roles.

Key teaching points
- Player 1 must focus on correct running form/mechanics and explosive drive
- Player 2 works *with* Player 1, allowing the Flexi-cord to provide the resistance

Sets and reps
1 set of 6 reps plus 1 contrast run with 30 seconds recovery between each rep and 3 minutes recovery before the next exercise.

Variations/progressions
- Lateral buggy run – Player 1 accelerates laterally for the first 2 yards before turning to cover the remaining distance linearly
- Players to carry sticks
- Perform resisted buggy-run dribbling drills
- Goalkeepers to wear kit

DRILL FLEXI-CORD – OUT AND BACK

Aim
To develop short, explosive, angled accelerated runs – ideal for beating an opponent to the ball or into a space.

Area/equipment
Large indoor or outdoor area of 10 square yards would be ideal. Place 5 cones as shown in fig 5.1(a), 1 Viper Belt with a Flexi-cord attached to 1 anchor point on the belt and a safety belt on the other end of the Flexi-cord.

Description
Work in pairs. Player 1 carries a stick and wears the Viper Belt. Player 2 stands directly behind Player 1 holding the Flexi-cord and wearing the safety belt. The Flexi-cord should be taut at this stage. Player 2 nominates a cone for Player 1, varying between the 3 cones for the required number of repetitions. Player 1 runs to the nominated cone, puts the stick to the floor as though receiving a ball or about to make a tackle, then returns to the start using short, sharp steps. Finish with a contrast run before swapping roles.

Key teaching points
- Focus on short, sharp explosive steps and a fast, powerful arm drive
- Maintain correct running form/mechanics
- Work off the balls of the feet
- Use short steps while returning to the start, and keep the weight forward

Sets and reps
3 sets of 6 reps plus 1 contrast run per set with 3 minutes recovery between each set. For advanced players, depending on the time of the season, increase to 10 reps.

Variations/progressions
- Perform the drill laterally
- Work backwards with short, sharp steps
- A third player or coach feeds a ball in to Player 1 at the cone, who must control it and pass it back
- Goalkeepers should wear kit and kick the ball back to Player 3

FLEXI-CORD – OUT AND BACK contd.

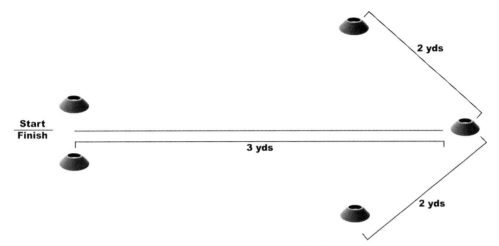

Start
Finish

2 yds

3 yds

2 yds

Figure 5.1(a) Flexi-cord out-and-back grid

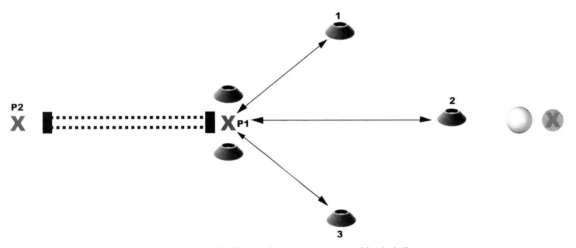

Figure 5.1(b) Flexi-cord resistance – out-and-back drill

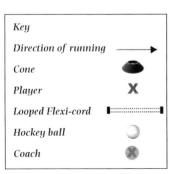

Key

Direction of running ⟶

Cone

Player   X

Looped Flexi-cord

Hockey ball

Coach

FLEXI-CORD –
DRILL LATERAL BALL WORK WITH PASS

Aim
To develop explosive lateral ability, control and accurate passing of the ball at speed when under pressure.

Area/equipment
Indoor or outdoor area. Viper Belt, Flexi-cords, hockey balls and 4 cones set up as shown in fig. 5.2.

Description
Player 1 is connected to players 2 and 3 by a Viper Belt and 2 Flexi-cords, 1 attached to either side of the belt worn by Player 1. Player 1 works laterally across to receive a ball that has been passed through the cones A/B by Player 4. Player 1 receives the pass, works laterally across and passes the ball back to Player 4 through cones C/D. The drill continues in this manner for the required number of sets and reps before the players swap roles.

Key teaching points
- Reassert good arm mechanics when possible
- Maintain correct running form/mechanics
- Use good technique for receiving, passing and dribbling
- Players 2 and 3 should not need to move, although they may need to move the Flexi-cord as Player 1 comes towards them

Sets and reps
3 sets of 8 reps plus 2 contrast runs and passes with 3 minutes recovery between each set.

Variations/progressions
- Increase the number of reps for advanced players
- Set up 2 identical drills opposite each other so that Player 1 is passing to another player who is working in the same way
- Goalkeepers are to wear kit, and kick the ball to each other

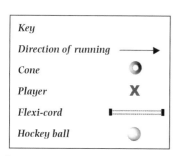

Key	
Direction of running	→
Cone	○
Player	X
Flexi-cord	▮·····▮
Hockey ball	◯

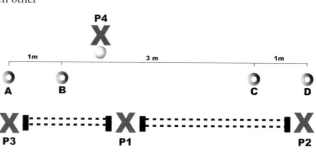

Figure 5.2 Flexi-cord – lateral ball work with pass

DRILL | *FLEXI-CORD – OVERSPEED*

Aim
To develop lightning-quick acceleration.

Area/equipment
Indoor or outdoor area; 4 cones and 1 Viper Belt with a Flexi-cord. Place the cones 3 yards apart in a T formation (*see* fig. 5.3).

Description
Work in pairs. Player 1 wears the Viper Belt and faces Player 2 who holds the flexi-cord and has the safety belt around his or her waist, i.e. the Flexi-cord will go from belly button to belly button. Player 1 stands at cone A, Player 2 stands at cone B and walks backwards away from Player 1, thereby increasing the cord's resistance. After stretching the cord for 4–5 yards, Player 1 accelerates towards Player 2 who then nominates cone C or D, requiring Player 1 to change direction explosively. Walk back to the start and repeat the drill.

Key teaching points
- Maintain correct running form/mechanics
- Control the running form/mechanics
- During the change of direction phase, shorten the steps and increase the rate of firing of the arms

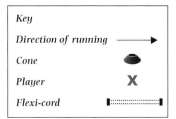

Sets and reps
3 sets of 8 reps plus 1 contrast run with 3 minutes recovery between each set.

Variations/progressions
- Player 1 starts with a horizontal jump before accelerating away
- Introduce a ball for the player to run on to after the change of direction phase
- Introduce a third player who receives the ball from Player 1 after he or she has picked it up

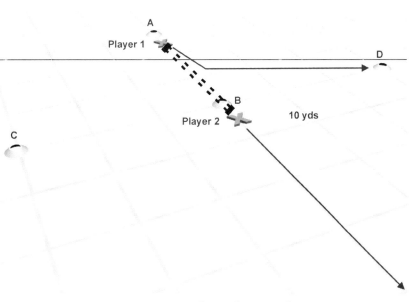

Figure 5.3 Flexi-cord – overspeed

DRILL | *FLEXI-CORD –*
ASSISTED/RESISTED TOW RUNS

Aim
To develop explosive speed with control.

Area/equipment
Large indoor or outdoor area and a Viper Belt.

Description
Players 1 and 2 are attached to one another by the Viper Belt. Player 1 runs away from Player 2 who stands still until pulled forwards. At this point Player 2, who is carrying a stick, accelerates after Player 1 who then begins to slow down to a stop. Simultaneously, Player 1 is performing a resisted drill and Player 2 an assisted drill.

Key teaching points
■ Maintain correct running form/mechanics
■ Both players should use a strong arm drive
■ Both players should use short, explosive steps during the acceleration phases
■ Player 2 (the assisted player) must keep an upward and forward lean and not try to resist the acceleration by leaning back

Sets and reps
2 sets of 4 reps (each player to complete 2 assisted and 2 resisted reps). Players should take 20 seconds recovery between each rep and 3 minutes between each set.

Variations/progressions
■ Introduce cones A and B so that Player 2 incorporates a swerve in to the run
■ Introduce hockey balls at the cones for Player 2 to accelerate on to
■ Introduce a third player/coach who feeds a ball in for Player 2 to accelerate on to

B

A

Key	
Direction of running	⟶
Cone	◯
Player	**X**
Flexi-cord	▮┄┄┄┄┄▮
Hockey ball	◯

Figure 5.4 Assisted and resisted tow runs

DRILL | *FLEXI-CORD –*
LATERAL SPEED DEVELOPMENT

Aim
To develop explosive, controlled and powerful lateral movements.

Area/equipment
An indoor or outdoor area; Viper Belt, cones, hockey stick and balls. Place 14 cones in two parallel lines about 3 yards apart, as shown in fig 5.5.

Description
Players 1 and 2 are connected by the Viper Belt with Player 1 working as the resisted player. Player 2 resists Player 1 from a lateral and backwards position (*see* fig. 5.5). Player 1 carries a stick and explodes laterally from cone A to cone B, then puts the stick to the floor as though making a tackle outside cone B. Player 1 moves laterally forwards with small, controlled recovery strides to cone C before exploding to cone D. Player 1 completes the entire length of the cones in this manner before walking back to the start to repeat the drill.

Key teaching points
■ Correct running form/mechanics to be used
■ Work off the balls of the feet
■ Use an explosive powerful arm drive
■ Keep the hips square
■ Player 2 to move along with Player 1 concentrating on maintaining a constant distance, angle and resistance.

Sets and rep
2 sets of 5 reps plus a contrast run per set with a walk-back recovery between each rep and 2 minutes recovery between sets. Set 1 is an open side-tackle and set 2 a reverse stick tackle.

Variations/progressions
Introduce a third player/coach who feeds a ball to Player 1 at the end of the explosive lateral phase that must be controlled and sent back.

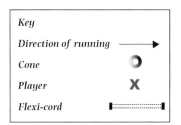

Key

Direction of running	⟶
Cone	◯
Player	**X**
Flexi-cord	▐┄┄┄┄┄▐

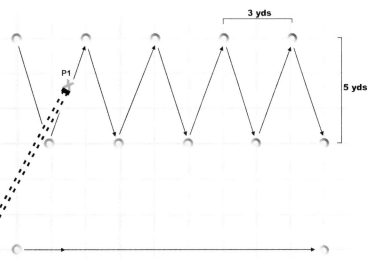

Figure 5.5 Lateral speed development resistance drill

FLEXI-CORD –
DRILL MULTI-DIRECTIONAL PASSING

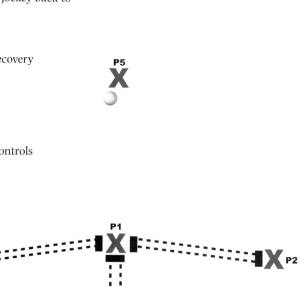

Aim

To develop explosive acceleration in all directions and at a variety of angles. To improve passing skills under pressure.

Area/equipment

An indoor or outdoor area; Viper Belt with 3 Flexi-cords attached, one on either side and one at the back; hockey balls and a stick.

Description

Player 1 wears the Viper Belt and is attached to Players 2, 3 and 4 by separate Flexi-cords. Player 5/coach feeds a ball into the area in front of Player 1 who explodes towards the ball, collects it, controls it and sends it back to Player 5 before jogging backwards to the start to repeat the drill.

Key teaching points

- Maintain correct running form/mechanics
- Use good arm drive when not on the ball
- Player 1 must use correct hockey techniques when on the ball
- Player 5/coach must give Player 1 adequate time to jockey back to the start between reps

Sets and reps

2 sets of 10 reps plus 2 contrast runs with 3 minutes recovery between each set.

Variations/progressions

- Player 5 to send a lifted ball to Player 1 to control
- Vary the type of pass performed by Player 1
- Perform the drill in the circle area so that Player 1 controls the ball before shooting at goal
- Goalkeepers to wear kit and to kick the ball back

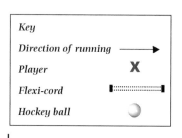

Figure 5.6 Resisted multi-directional explosive passing

DRILL *SIDE STEPPER – RESISTED LATERAL RUNS*

Aim
To develop explosive, controlled lateral patterns of running.

Area/equipment
Indoor or outdoor area; Side-Stepper. Place 10–12 cones placed in a zigzag pattern (*see* fig. 5.7).

Description
The player wearing the Side Stepper runs in a lateral zigzag between the cones, down the length of the grid and just before a cone, extends the last step to increase the level of resistance; then turns round and works back along the grid.

Key teaching points
- Maintain correct lateral running form/mechanics
- Do not sink into the hips when stepping off to change direction
- During the directional change phase, increase arm speed to provide additional control

Sets and reps
3 sets of 6 reps plus 1 contrast run with 3 minutes recovery between each set.

Variations/progressions
- Perform the drill backwards
- Include a stick, which is to be placed down on arrival at each cone
- Introduce a ball
- Goalkeepers to wear kit

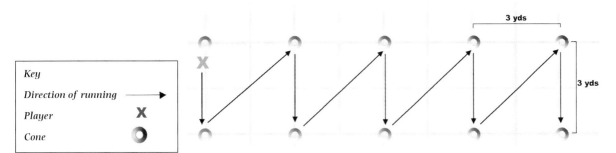

Figure 5.7 Side-Stepper resisted lateral runs

DRILL · SIDE STEPPER – JOCKEYING IN PAIRS

Aim

To develop one-to-one marking skills with particular focus on defensive and attacking movement.

Area/equipment

Indoor or outdoor area; 6-8 cones mark out a channel about 20 yards long and 3 yards wide (*see* fig. 5.8); Side-Steppers.

Description

Both players wear a Side Stepper and face each other about 2 yards apart. The attacking player (1) moves from right to left in a backwards pattern while the defending player (2) attempts to mirror the movements to prevent Player 1 from having too much space, i.e. Player 1 works forward and Player 2 backwards.

Key teaching points

- Use quick, low steps *not* high knees
- Do not skip or jump – one foot should be in contact with the floor at all times
- Try to keep the feet shoulder-width apart
- Use a powerful arm drive
- Do not sink into the hips

Sets and reps

3 sets of 4 reps with 30 seconds recovery between each rep and 2 minutes recovery between each set. Players to swap roles after each rep.

Variations/progressions

- Both players perform the drill laterally, one player leading and the other trying to mirror
- Introduce sticks and balls

Key	
Direction of running	→
Cone	◎
Player	X
Hockey ball	◯

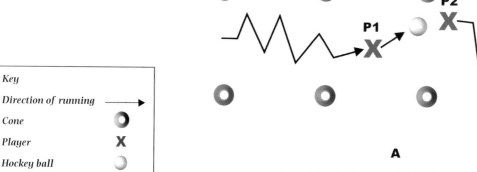

A

Figure 5.8 Side-Stepper resisted jockeying in pairs

DRILL *HAND-WEIGHT DROPS*

Aim
To develop explosive power, re-acceleration and, specifically, a powerful arm drive.

Area/equipment
Indoor or outdoor area; 3 cones, and hand-weights of 2–4 lb. Place 1 cone to represent the start, a second 15 yards away and the third 10 yards away from the second.

Description
The player carrying the weights accelerates to the second cone and releases them – keeping a natural flow to the arm mechanics – then continues to accelerate to the third cone before decelerating and walking back to the start. The drill is repeated.

Key teaching points
- Maintain correct running form/mechanics
- Do not stop the arm drive to release the weights
- Do not stop and/or look to see what has happened to the weights on release
- Quality not quantity is vital

Sets and reps
3 sets of 4 reps with 3 minutes recovery between each set.

Variations/progressions
- On the release of the weights the coach calls a change of direction, i.e. the player is to accelerate off at different angles
- Perform the drill backwards over the first 15 yards then turn, accelerate and release the weights to explode away
- Perform the drill laterally over the first 15 yards then turn, accelerate and release the weights to explode away

DRILL | PARACHUTE RUNNING

Aim
To develop explosive running over longer distances (sprint endurance) and explosive acceleration.

Area/equipment
Indoor or outdoor area; 4 cones and a parachute. Mark out a grid 50 yards long, place one cone as a start marker, one at a distance of 30 yards, one at 40 yards and one at 50 yards from the start.

Description
A player wearing the parachute accelerates to the 40-yard cone then decelerates.

Key teaching points
- Maintain correct running form/mechanics
- Do not worry if, with the wind and the resistance, you feel as though you are being pulled from side to side, this will improve your balance and co-ordination
- Do not lean into the run too much
- Quality not quantity is vital

Sets and reps
3 sets of 5 reps plus 1 contrast run with a walk-back recovery between each rep and 3 minutes recovery between each set.

Variations/progressions
- Explosive acceleration: the parachutes have a release mechanism; the player accelerates to the 30-yard cone, releases the parachute and explodes to the 40-yard cone before decelerating
- Introduce a stick to be carried while repeating the above progression
- Random change of direction: the coach stands behind the 30-yard cone, and, as the player releases the parachute, indicates a change in the direction of the run
- The coach introduces a ball for players to run on to during the explosive phase
- When the above drill is mastered the ball can be fed in by the coach to encourage the player to accelerate on to a moving ball

DRILL BALL DROPS

Aim
To develop explosive reactions.

Area/equipment
Indoor or outdoor area; 1 or 2 tennis balls.

Description
Work in pairs. One player drops the ball at various distances and angles from his or her partner. The ball is dropped from shoulder height and immediately the partner explodes forwards and attempts to catch the ball before the second bounce. (Distances between players will differ because the height of the bounce will vary depending on the ground surface.)

Key teaching points
- Work off the balls of the feet, particularly prior to the drop
- Use a very explosive arm drive
- The initial steps should be short, fast and explosive
- At the take-off do not jump, dither or hesitate
- Work on developing a smooth one-movement run

Sets and reps
3 sets of 10 reps with 2 minutes recovery between each set.

Variations/progressions
- Player to hold 2 balls and to drop just 1
- Work in groups of 3 with 2 of the players at different angles alternately dropping a ball for the third player to catch; on achieving this, the player turns and accelerates away to catch/dive on the second ball
- Alter the start positions, e.g. sideways, backwards with a call, seated, etc.

DRILL UPHILL RUNS

Aim
To develop sprint endurance and explosive running.

Area/equipment
The hill should be 20–80 yards in length with a gradient of no more than 8°. A few cones can be used to mark out various distances.

Description
Players are to accelerate up the hill over the nominated distance and perform a slow jog or walk back to the start before repeating the drill.

Key teaching points
- Maintain correct running form/mechanics
- Ensure that a strong knee and arm drive are used
- Work at maximal effort
- Adequate recovery time between reps is essential
- Do not attempt to run up hills with steep gradients as this will have a negative impact on the running mechanics

Sets and reps
3 sets of 6 reps with a jog- or walk-back recovery between reps and 3 minutes recovery between sets.

Variations/progressions
- Accelerate over the initial few yards backwards before turning to complete the drill as above
- Overspeed – accelerate down the hill (NB: Control is vital!)

DRILL BREAK-AWAY MIRROR DRILLS

Aim
To develop multi-directional explosive reactions.

Area/equipment
Indoor or outdoor area; 1 Break-Away Belt.

Description
Work in pairs, and face each other attached by the Break-Away Belt. Set a time limit. Player 1 is the proactive player while Player 2 is reactive. Player 1 attempts to get away from Player 2 by using either sideways, forwards or backwards movements. Players are not allowed to turn round and run away. The drill ends if and when the proactive player breaks the belt connection or the time runs out.

Key teaching points
- Stay focused on your partner
- Do not sink into the hips
- Keep the head tall and the spine straight
- Maintain correct arm mechanics

Sets and reps
3 sets where 1 set = 30 seconds of each player taking the proactive role followed by a 1 minute recovery period.

Variations/progressions
Side-by-side mirror drills – the object is for the proactive player to move away laterally and gain as much distance as possible before the other can react.

DRILL MEDICINE BALL (JELLY BALL) WORKOUT

Aim
To develop explosive upper body and core power.

Area/equipment
Indoor or outdoor area; jelly balls of various weights from 4 to 18 lb.

Description
Work in pairs. The players perform simple throws, e.g. chest passes, single-arm passes, front slams, back slams, twist passes, side throws, woodchopper and granny throws.

Key teaching points
■ Start with a lighter ball as a warm-up set
■ Start with simple movements first before progressing to twists etc.
■ Keep the spine in an upright position
■ Take care when loading (catching) and unloading (throwing) as this can put stress on the lower back

Sets and reps
1 set of 12 reps of each drill with 1 minute recovery between each drill and 3 minutes recovery before the next exercise.

DRILL *SLED RUNNING*

Aim
To develop explosive sprint endurance.

Area/equipment
Large outdoor grass area; cones and sprint sled. Mark out an area of 30–60 yards.

Description
The player is connected to the sled and sprints over the nominated distance before recovering, turning around and repeating the drill.

Key teaching points
- Maintain correct running form/mechanics
- Maintain a strong arm drive
- Often players will need to use an exaggerated lean to initiate the momentum required to get the sled moving
- As momentum picks up, the player should transfer to the correct running position

Sets and reps
2 sets of 5 reps plus 1 contrast run with 1 minute recovery between each rep and 3 minutes recovery between each set.

Variations/progressions
5-yard explosive acceleration – the player covers 50 yards by alternating between acceleration and deceleration phases over distances of 5 yards. (NB: Quality and not quantity is the key here!)

DRILL   PLYOMETRICS – LOW-IMPACT QUICK JUMP.

Aim
To develop explosive power for running, jumping and changing direction.

Area/equipment
Indoor or outdoor area; Fast Foot Ladder or cones placed 18 inches apart.

Description
The player performs double-footed single jumps, i.e. 1 jump between each rung (*see* fig. 5.9(a)). On reaching the end of the ladder, the player turns round and jumps back.

Key teaching points
- Maintain correct jumping form/mechanics
- The emphasis is on the speed of the jumps *not* the height
- Start slowly and increase the speed but do not lose control, i.e. avoid feeling as though you are about to fall over the edge of a cliff when you reach the end of the drill
- Do not lean forwards too much

Sets and reps
2 sets of 2 reps with 1 minute recovery between each set.

Variations/progressions
- Backwards jumps
- Two jumps forward and one back (*see* fig. 5.9(b))
- Sideways jumps
- Sideways jumps, two forwards and one back
- Hopscotch – 2 feet in the square and then 1 foot either side of the next square
- Left- and right-footed hops
- Increase the intensity – replace ladders or cones with 7–12-inch hurdles and perform the drills above

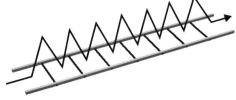

Figure 5.9(a) Plyometrics – low-impact, quick jumps

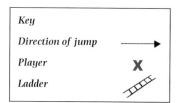

Key	
Direction of jump	→
Player	**X**
Ladder	

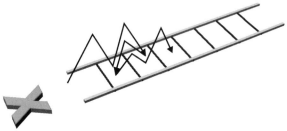

Figure 5.9(b) Plyometrics – two jumps forward and one back

DRILL   *PLYOMETRIC CIRCUIT*

Aim
To develop explosive multi-directional speed, agility and quickness.

Area/equipment
Indoor or outdoor area. Place ladders, hurdles and cones in a circuit formation (*see* fig. 5.10).

Description
The players are to jump, hop and zigzag their way through the circuit as stipulated by the coach.

Key teaching points
■ Maintain the correct mechanics for each part of the circuit
■ Ensure that there is a smooth transfer from running to jumping movements and vice versa

Sets and reps
5 circuits with 1 minute recovery between each circuit.

Variations/progressions
Work in pairs. Player 1 completes the circuit while Player 2 feeds the ball in at various points around the circuit for Player 1 to pass back.

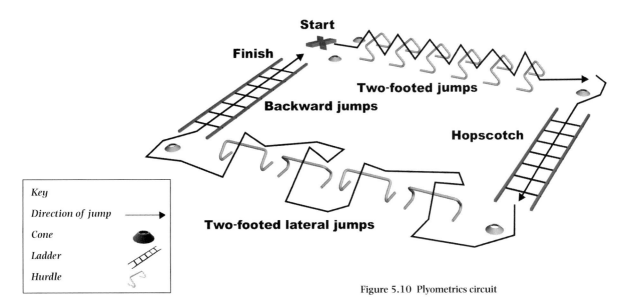

Figure 5.10 Plyometrics circuit

DRILL PLYOMETRICS – DROP-JUMPS

Aim
To develop explosive multi-directional speed.

Area/equipment
Indoor or outdoor area with a cushioned or grassed landing surface; a stable platform or bench to jump from of variable height 15–36 inches depending on the stage in the season.

Description
The player stands on the platform and jumps off with feet together, lands on the balls of the feet then accelerates away for 5 yards.

Key teaching points
- Do not land flat-footed
- Do not sink into the hips on landing
- Maintain a strong core
- Keep the head up – this will help align the spine

Sets and reps
2 sets of 10 reps with 3 minutes recovery between each set.

Variations/progressions
- Backward drop-jumps
- Side drop-jumps
- Drop-jumps with a mid-air twist
- Include a ball for the players to accelerate on to

CHAPTER 6

EXPRESSION OF POTENTIAL

TEAM GAMES IN PREPARATION FOR THE NEXT LEVEL

This stage is quite short in duration, but very important, bringing together all the elements of the continuum into a highly competitive situation involving other players. Short, high-intensity tag-type games and random agility tests work well here.

The key is for players to be fired up – to perform fast, explosive and controlled movements that leave them exhilarated – mentally and physically ready for the next stage in training or the game on Saturday.

DRILL   'BRITISH BULLDOG'

Aim
To practise multi-directional explosive movements in a pressure situation.

Area/equipment
Outdoor or indoor area of about 20 square yards; about 20 cones to mark start and finish.

Description
One player is nominated and situated in the centre of the grid, the rest of the players stand at one side. On the coach's call all the players attempt to get to the opposite side of the square without being caught by the player in the middle. When the player in the middle captures another player, he or she joins the first player and helps to capture more prisoners.

Key teaching points
▪ Correct mechanics are used at all times
▪ All players must keep their heads and eyes up to avoid collisions

Sets and reps
Play British Bulldog for about 3-4 minutes before moving on to the more technical aspects of the game.

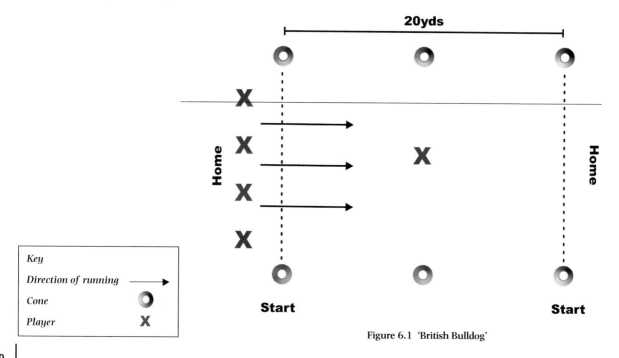

Figure 6.1 'British Bulldog'

DRILL   *CIRCLE BALL*

Aim
To practise using explosive evasion skills.

Area/equipment
Outdoor or indoor area. Players make a circle of about 15 yards in diameter (depending on the size of the squad); tennis balls.

Description
One or two players stand in the centre of the circle while the players on the outside have 1 or 2 balls. The players on the outside try to make ball contact with the players on the inside, who in turn try to dodge the ball. The winners are the pair with the least number of hits during their turn in the centre.

Key teaching points
The players in the middle should use the correct mechanics.

Sets and reps
Each pair should stay in the centre area for 45 seconds.

Variations/progressions
Players in the middle have to hold on to each other.

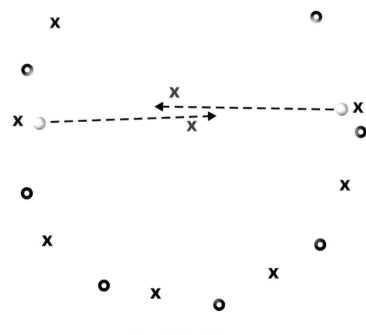

Figure 6.2 Circle ball

DRILL 'ROBBING THE NEST'

Aim
To practise multi-directional explosive speed, agility and quickness.

Area/equipment
Outdoor or indoor area of about 20 square yards with a centre circle marked out with cones measuring 2 yards in diameter. Place a number of balls in the centre circle.

Description
Two nominated players protect the nest of balls with the rest of the players standing outside the square area. The game starts when the outside players run in and try to steal the balls from the nest by dribbling to the outside (safe) zone of the square. The two defenders try to prevent this by stopping the robbers with a fair tackle. For every successful tackle, the ball is returned to the centre circle.

Key teaching points
▨ Correct mechanics must be used at all times
▨ Players should dodge, swerve, weave, sidestep, etc.

Sets and reps
Each pair to defend for about 45 seconds.

Key	
Direction of running	⟶
Cone	◉
Player	X
Ball	◯

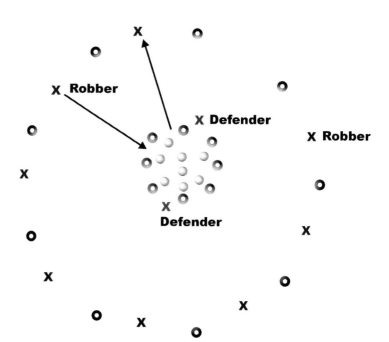

Figure 6.3 'Robbing the nest'

| DRILL | **ODD ONE OUT** |

Aim
To practise speed, agility and quickness in a competitive environment.

Area/equipment
Outdoor or indoor area; cones and balls. Mark out a circle of 20–25 yards in diameter and a centre circle of about 2 yards in diameter.

Description
Place a number of balls in the centre area, one less than the number of players. The players stand on the outside of the larger circle; on the coach's call, they start running around the larger circle. On the coach's second call they collect a ball from the centre circle as quickly as possible. The player who fails is the odd man out and performs a hockey skill drill as directed by the coach. Another ball is removed and the process repeated.

Key teaching points
- Correct mechanics must be used at all times
- Players must be aware of the other players around them

Sets and reps
Play the game until a winner emerges.

Variations/progressions
Work in pairs, i.e. one ball between two players.

Key	
Direction of ball	→
Cone	◉
Player	**X**
Ball	◗

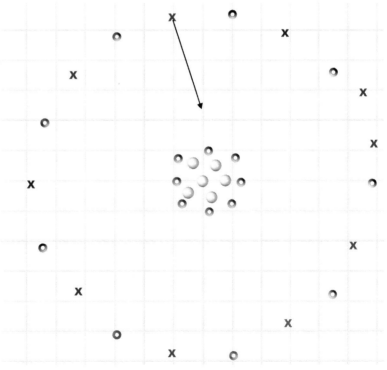

Figure 6.4 Odd one out

DRILL CONE TURNS

Aim
To practise multi-directional speed, agility and quickness.

Area/equipment
Outdoor or indoor area of about 20 square yards and 50 small cone markers. Place the cones in and around the grid; 25 of the cones should be turned upside down.

Description
Work in two small teams (2–3 players). One team attempts to turn over the upright cones and the other attempts to turn over the upside-down cones. The winning team is the one to have the largest number of cones its own way up within the prescribed time.

Key teaching points
- Players must initiate good arm drive after turning a cone
- Players must correct multi-directional mechanics
- Players must be aware of others around the area

Sets and reps
A game should last for 60 seconds.

Variations/progressions
Use 4 teams and allocate 4 different-coloured cones.

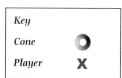

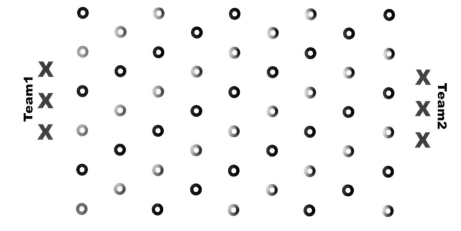

Figure 6.5 Cone turns

DRILL SMALL TEAMS – KEEPING THE BALL

Aim
To practise multi-directional speed, agility and quickness in game-like situations.

Area/equipment
Indoor or outdoor area, the size of which will be dependent on the number of players involved.

Description
Organise teams of 3 a side in a limited area where the aim is for each team to maintain possession of the ball for as long as possible. When a team loses possession or allows the ball to go out of the designated area the opposing team gains and attempts to keep it.

Key teaching points
- Good communication between players is important
- Correct passing, dribbling and tackling techniques are to be used
- Keep the head and eyes up as much as possible
- Use short, sharp, explosive movements to create and utilise space

Sets and reps
Play for short periods, about 3 minutes.

Variations/progressions
- 3 v. 2
- 2 v. 1
- Introduce a variety of conditions such as: push passes only; two touches only; no verbal communication

CHAPTER 7 POSITION–SPECIFIC DRILLS

This section provides examples not just of hockey-specific but also of position-specific patterns of movement. It looks at combining all the areas of the SAQ Continuum – including techniques, equipment and drills – into game- and position-specific situations to improve and perfect the movement skills required by players for optimal performance.

The primary aim is to improve the multi-directional explosive speed, agility, control, power and co-ordination required by hockey players in all areas of the pitch. These drills are best introduced when the foundation work of SAQ Training has been mastered and during training sessions where attention is being given to position-specific movements.

DRILL | *POSITION – ALL PLAYERS*
EYE–HAND, VISUAL ACUITY

Aim
To develop fast accurate catching skills. To develop the players' visual skills in following the ball in flight.

Area/equipment
Outdoor or indoor area; Visual Acuity Ring.

Description
Work in pairs about 5 yards apart. The ring is tossed so that it rotates through the air and is caught by the player on the colour nominated by the coach.

Key teaching points
■ Keep the head still – move the eyes to track the ring
■ Work off the balls of the feet at all times
■ The hands should be out and in front of the body ready to catch the ring

Sets and reps
2 sets of 20 reps with 1 minute recovery between each set.

Variations/progressions
Turn and catch.

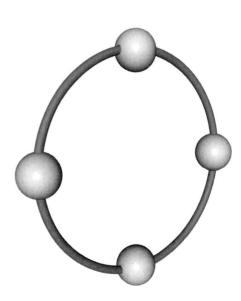

Figure 7.1 Visual Acuity Ring

DRILL *PERIPHERAL AWARENESS*

Aim

To develop peripheral awareness. To help the players detect and react more quickly to the ball coming at them from all angles.

Area/equipment

Outdoor or indoor area; Peripheral Vision Stick.

Description

Work in pairs with Player 2 behind the active player (1) who stands in a ready position. Player 2 holds the stick and moves it from behind Player 1 into his or her field of vision. As soon as Player 1 detects the stick he or she claps both hands over the ball at the end of the stick.

Key teaching points

- Player 1 should work off the balls of the feet and in a slightly crouched position with the hands out ready
- Player 2 must be careful not to touch any part of Player 1's body with the stick
- Player 2 should vary the speed at which the stick is brought into Player 1's field of vision

Sets and reps

2 set of 20 reps with no recovery between each rep and a 1 minute recovery between each set.

Variations/progressions

Instead of using a vision stick, throw balls from behind Player 1 to be fended off.

Figure 7.2 Peripheral Vision Stick

DRILL | **POSITION – ALL PLAYERS**
BUNT BAT

Aim
To develop lightning-quick hand–eye co-ordination.

Area/equipment
Outdoor or indoor area. A Bunt Bat and tennis balls or bean bags.

Description
Work in pairs, one of the players holding the Bunt Bat. The partner stands about 3–4 yards away and throws a ball or bean bag, simultaneously calling the colour of a ball on the Bunt Bat. The player's task is to fend off the ball or bean bag with the appropriate coloured ball on the Bunt Bat.

Key teaching points
- Start throwing the balls or bean bags slowly and gradually build up the speed
- Player should be in a get-set position

Sets and reps
3 sets of 25 reps with 30 seconds recovery between each set.

Variations/progressions
- Use different-coloured balls or bean bags – the ball or bean bag is to be fended off with the corresponding coloured ball on the Bunt Bat
- Stand on an agility disc while using the Bunt Bat.

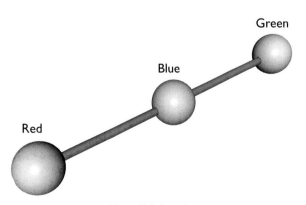

Green

Blue

Red

Figure 7.3 Bunt Bat

DRILL | *OUT AND OUT AGAIN*

Aim

To develop a player's ability to threaten an opponent in a low, controlled manner and to force an error or win the ball.

Area/equipment

Indoor or outdoor area; Viper Belt, Flexi-cord and hockey balls.

Description

Player 1 is connected to Player 2 with the Flexi-cord. Player 1 threatens Player 3 – the opposition player on the ball – and attempts to make Player 3 move. As Player 3 moves the ball, Player 1 steps forward again to win the ball or force an error. Player 1 jockeys back to the start before repeating the drill. (*See* fig. 7.4.)

Key teaching points

■ Good hockey technique must be used by all players
■ Player 1 should stay low throughout both phases
■ Player 1 should use short steps and not over-commit
■ Keep the head and eyes up for good vision

Sets and reps

2 sets of 6–10 reps plus 2 contrast runs with 15 seconds rest between reps and 3 minutes recovery between each set.

Variations/progressions

■ Player 3 to become increasingly active in the role
■ Player 1 to make a square pass having won the ball for Player 2 to explode on to

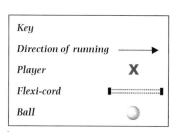

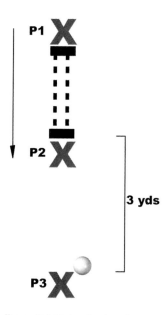

Figure 7.4 Out and out again

DRILL | *POSITION – ALL PLAYERS*
PRESSING THE BALL

Aim
To develop the ability to press the ball and opposition, closing down the space and therefore the options that the opposition has.

Area/equipment
Indoor or outdoor area. For maximum impact perform the drill in relevant positions on the pitch. Use light hand-weights and 8 cones placed as shown in fig. 7.5.

Description
Player 1, holding the hand-weights, starts between cones A and B, his or her back to the other cones, and moves laterally and continuously between them. The coach nominates one of the cones 1–6 to represent the ball or opponent. The player turns, accelerates away and drops the hand-weights after 4 or 5 strides, exploding towards the nominated cone.

Key teaching points
- Maintain correct running form/mechanics
- Use short, fast steps and a good arm drive particularly on the turn
- Try to drop the hand-weights in stride – do not throw or hesitate to release them

Sets and reps
3 sets of 5 reps with a walk-back recovery between reps and 2 minutes recovery between sets.

Variations/progressions
Replace the cones with players and hockey balls so that as Player 1 turns, one of the other players becomes active so that Player 1 has to close him or her down and attempt to win the ball.

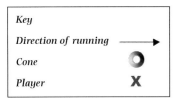

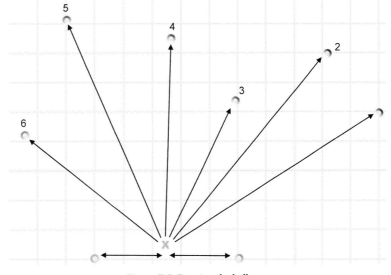

Figure 7.5 Pressing the ball

POSITION – ALL PLAYERS

DRILL   TURN AND CHASE

Aim

To react instantly to loss of possession and work back to a strong position on the pitch.

Area/equipment

Large indoor or outdoor area; 2 sections of 7½-foot Fast Foot Ladder, hockey balls and cones positioned as shown in fig. 7.6.

Description

Player 1 carries a stick and fires down the first ladder, picks up the ball at the end and accelerates across the middle area. On reaching the second ladder Player 1 leaves (loses) the ball and uses the second ladder to decelerate. Immediately on leaving the second ladder, Player 1 turns to chase Player 2 who attempts to dribble the ball to the cone before Player 1 can retrieve it.

Key teaching points

■ Ensure that correct running technique is used when off the ball
■ Ensure that good hockey technique is used when on the ball
■ Players are to turn to either side off the end of the second ladder
■ Players are to retreat as quickly and as efficiently as possible to the cone

Sets and reps

2 sets of 5–8 reps with a walk-back recovery between reps and 3 minutes recovery between each set.

Variations/progressions

■ Introduce a swerve-run course or dodge for Player 1 to perform in the middle area
■ Vary the position on the pitch where the drill is performed
■ Introduce Player 3 who closes down Player 2 and forces or channels him or her wide and away from the cone while Player 1 is chasing back

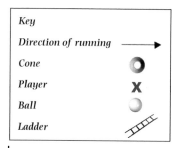

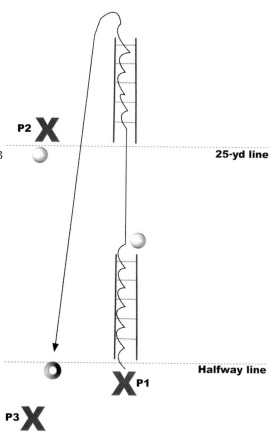

Figure 7.6 Lose possession, turn and chase

POSITION – DEFENCE
DRILL ALIGNMENT AND COMMUNICATION

Aim
To develop positional awareness, speed, co-ordination and communication between defensive players.

Area/equipment
Large indoor or outdoor area; 2 Break-Away Belts and 12 cones (3 of 4 different colours). Mark out an area of 10 square yards with 3 cones of the same colour 1 yard apart on each side of the square (*see* fig. 7.7).

Description
Three players are joined together by the 2 Break-Away Belts, i.e. with the player in the middle attached to the player on the left and the right. On the coach's call the players move to a set of coloured cones and touch one cone each without breaking the belts. The coach immediately calls another set of cones either behind or to the side. The players then move to touch these cones without breaking the belts.

Key teaching points
- Maintain correct running form/mechanics
- Players should use a strong arm drive particularly when changing direction
- Do not cross the feet or skip when changing direction
- There should be good communication between players

Sets and reps
3 sets of 8 reps (calls from coach) with 2 minutes rest between sets.

Variations/progressions
Set up a hexagon grid using 18 cones (3 of 6 different colours).

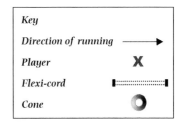

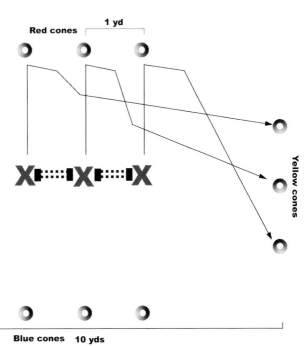

Figure 7.7 Alignment and communication defence drill

POSITION – DEFENCE
DRILL LOW DEFENSIVE POSITION

Aim

To develop the ability of players to maintain a dynamic, solid low defensive position for prolonged periods of time.

Area/equipment

Indoor or outdoor area; cones, metal or wooden stakes or poles and 20–25 yards of thin cord. Place the stakes or poles in a 4-yard square and tie the cord around the posts and then from corner to corner with the cord about 4 feet off the floor. Place cones in a W formation (*see* fig. 7.8).

Description

A player starts at one of the poles on the start line and accelerates towards cone 1, runs backwards to cone 2, forwards to cone 3, etc. The drill is completed when the player is back at the start. Rest for 20–30 seconds before repeating the drill in the opposite direction.

Key teaching points

- Players should keep their heads up
- Use short, sharp steps particularly when changing direction
- Work off the balls of the feet
- Keep the weight on the ball of the foot when moving backwards
- Use a strong arm drive

Key	
Cone	◎
Posts	●
Cord	··········

Sets and reps

2 sets of 6 with 20–30 seconds recovery between each rep and 2 minutes recovery between sets.

Variations/progressions

- Introduce a second player and a Viper Belt so that the drill is performed under resistance
- Introduce a second player with a ball who works around the W while the defensive player mirrors the movement
- Introduce a third player and combine the above two variations
- Vary the agility drill performed by Player 1

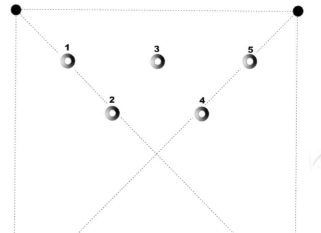

Figure 7.8 Low defensive position development

POSITION – DEFENCE

| DRILL | *HUNTING IN PAIRS* |

Aim
To encourage defensive players to work closely with one another and to prevent gaps opening up that an attacking player might exploit.

Area/equipment
Indoor or outdoor area; Break-Away Belt and hockey balls. Use cones to mark out an area of 5–10 square yards depending on the level of the group.

Description
Players 1 and 2 carry sticks and are connected by a Break-Away Belt. Player 3 (the opposition) is on the ball and aims to get from one end of the grid to the other. Players 1 and 2 work together to try to gain possession or to force the ball out of play without the belt connection breaking. The drill is over when either Player 1 and 2 gains possession, Player 3 gets to the other end of the grid or the ball goes out of play. (*See* fig. 7.9.)

Key teaching points
- Players 1 and 2 should communicate well
- Players 1 and 2 should force Player 3 into a chosen area
- Produce quality work at match pace
- Correct tackling techniques are to be used as appropriate

Sets and reps
3 sets of 6 reps with 60 seconds recovery between sets.

Variations/progressions
Introduce Player 4 who joins Player 3 to make a 2 v. 2 situation.

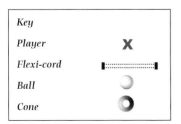

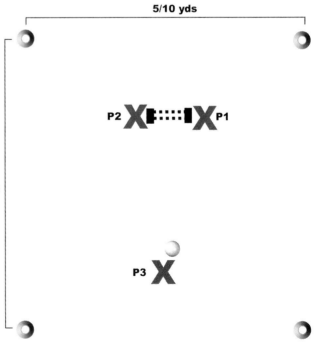

Figure 7.9 Hunting in pairs

DRILL | *TACKLING DRILL*

Aim

To develop the ability of defensive players to threaten and perform tackles in a controlled explosive manner

Area/equipment

Indoor or outdoor area of about 4 square yards – Side-Steppers and hockey balls.

Description

Player 1 (the defensive player) wears the Side-Stepper and attempts to take the ball in a legitimate manner from Player 2 who is moving around the area with the ball. Player 2 is allowed to move in any direction but may not turn his or her back on Player 1. Player 1 has 10–20 seconds in which to win the ball before changing roles with Player 2.

Key teaching points

- Use short, sharp steps with one foot in contact with the ground at all times
- Hold the stick in a technically correct way for tackling
- Player 1 should threaten Player 2 to try to force an error rather than always going straight in for the tackle

Sets and reps

Each player to perform 6 reps in the defensive and 6 in the attacking role with the changeover as the rest and recovery period.

Variations/progressions

Vary the size of the area and the time limit depending on the experience of the players involved to make the drill harder or easier as necessary.

POSITION – MIDFIELD

DRILL	*TURN, CHASE BACK AND COVER*

Aim

This drill is designed specifically for midfield players who will often find that the ball has been played in behind them and that they are required to turn and chase back to cover.

Area/equipment

Indoor or outdoor area (but for maximum impact perform the drill in a relevant area of the pitch); 12 cones and a Viper Belt with a hand leash attachment. Place the cones in a fan formation (*see* fig. 7.10).

Description

Work in pairs with Player 1 wearing the Viper Belt and facing Player 2 who is holding on to the hand leash. Player 1 moves backwards to the nominated cone 1–4 with Player 2 providing resistance. Upon reaching the first cone Player 2 releases Player 1 who turns and accelerates away to the nominated cone (5–12) on the outside of the fan.

Key teaching points

- Keep the weight forwards and work off the balls of the feet when moving backwards
- Use a strong arm drive
- Use short, sharp steps particularly on the turn
- Try to avoid crossing the feet over
- Assert correct running form/mechanics as quickly as possible after the turn

Sets and reps

2 sets of 6 reps with a walk-back recovery between each rep and 2 minutes recovery between sets.

Variations/progressions

- As Player 1 is released a ball is fed to a cone for the player to explode on to
- Introduce Player 3 who moves between the outside cones dribbling a ball. As Player 1 turns he or she closes Player 3 down and attempts to win the ball; Player 3 tries to beat Player 1.

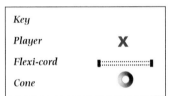

Key	
Player	**X**
Flexi-cord	▯ ᠁᠁᠁᠁ ▯
Cone	◉

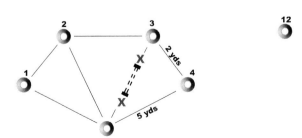

Figure 7.10 Turn, chase back and cover

MIDFIELD/FORWARD

DRILL SQUARE LAY-OFF AND SUPPORT

Aim

To develop explosive turning and running to support a lay-off pass (made by a midfield or forward player who has picked the ball up facing his or her own goal).

Area/equipment

Indoor or outdoor area but for maximum impact perform the drill in the attacking third of the pitch.

Description

Player 1, carrying stick and hand-weights, starts at cone A, moves towards cone B and picks up a ball passed from Player 2 who is at cone C. Having delivered the pass Player 2 accelerates in an arc around cone D or E to receive the ball back from Player 1. Player 1 then turns explosively and accelerates down the middle of the grid towards the goal. After about 5 yards Player 1 releases the hand-weights and explodes on to the ball that Player 2 has released into his or her path. Player 1 collects the ball and shoots at goal. (*See* fig. 7.11.)

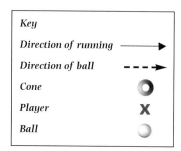

Key teaching points

- Focus on short, sharp steps particularly when turning
- There should be good communication between players
- Produce quality work at match pace
- Correct passing, receiving and shooting techniques are to be used by both players

Sets and reps

1 set of 8 reps with a walk-back recovery between reps.

Variations/progressions

- Player 2 also carries hand-weights to work on explosion
- Introduce Player 3 who times the run to arrive at the far post for a potential deflection from Player 1's shot

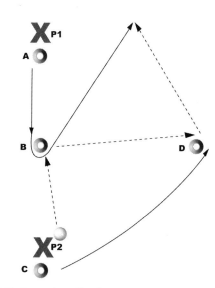

Figure 7.11 Square lay-off and support run

POSITION – MIDFIELD/FORWARD

| **DRILL** | **ROLLING OFF** |

Aim

To develop a player's ability to 'roll' off an opponent and accelerate away.

Area/equipment

Indoor or outdoor area but for maximum impact perform the drill in a relevant area of the pitch. Place 8 cones in a zigzag formation (*see* fig. 7.12) with a further 3 cones of different colours at various angles off the end of the zigzag channel.

Description

Player 1 carries a stick and accelerates towards cone A where he or she drops the left shoulder towards the cone and spins or rolls around to face cone B. Player 1 then accelerates to cone B dips the right shoulder towards the cone, rolls and accelerates on to cone C. Player 1 continues down the channel in this manner – at a random point Player 1 calls for a pass from Player 2. On receiving the pass Player 1 turns and accelerates to either the red, blue or green cone as directed by the coach.

Key teaching points

- Ensure that Player 2 is ready to make the pass
- Player 1 should use small steps on the turns
- Player 2 should make quality passes
- There should be good communication between players
- Encourage Player 2 to let the ball come as far past them as possible on receipt to improve the efficiency of the turn
- Player 1 should accelerate away as quickly as possible

Sets and reps

2 sets of 10 reps with a walk-back recovery between each rep and 2 minutes recovery between sets.

Variations/progressions

Introduce Player 3 who acts as a defender and marks Player 1 down the channel.

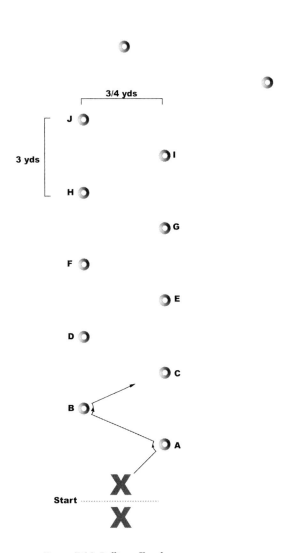

Figure 7.12 Rolling off a player

POSITION – MIDFIELD/FORWARD

DRILL ACCELERATE, DECELERATE, CHANGE DIRECTION

Aim
To develop off-the-mark acceleration, explosive swerves and controlled deceleration before changing direction.

Area/equipment
Large indoor or outdoor area; 2 Fast Foot Ladders and 7 cones set up as shown in fig. 7.13.

Description
Player 1 accelerates down the first ladder then accelerates and swerve-runs between the cones for 15 yards. On reaching the second ladder, Player 1 decelerates with control. The coach then nominates cone A, B or C, whereupon the player changes direction and accelerates to that cone where he or she receives a pass or makes a tackle or a pass.

Key teaching points
- Maintain correct running form/mechanics
- Lean back and fire the arms during the deceleration phase *but* players must stay on the balls of their feet
- During the change of direction phase stay tall, do not sink into the hips
- Do not cross the feet or skip

Sets and reps
1 set of 6 reps with a walk-back recovery between each rep and 3 minutes recovery before the next drill.

Variations/progressions
On the first ladder vary the Fast Foot Ladder drills, e.g. icky shuffle, lateral, etc.

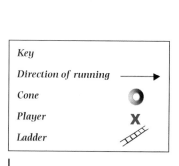

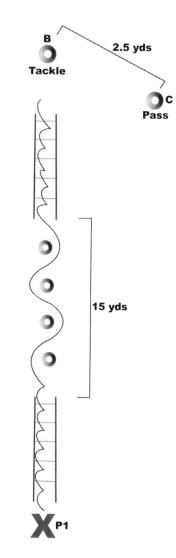

Figure 7.13 Accelerate, swerve, decelerate and change direction

POSITION – MIDFIELD/FORWARD

DRILL	**TOW RUNS WITH SWERVES**

Aim
To develop explosive speed and control while swerve-running.

Area/equipment
Large indoor or outdoor area (for maximum benefit perform the drill in the relevant areas of the pitch, i.e. near the sideline); 2 Viper Belts, 2 Flexi-cords and 5 cones in a straight line 5 yards apart.

Description
Players 1 and 2 are connected by the Viper Belts and both Flexi-cords. Player 1 accelerates from the first cone around the second. Player 2 remains stationary (so that Player 1 is resisted for the first 2 yards) until Player 1 has moved 2 yards away; due to the Flexi-cords Player 2 will then explode in pursuit of Player 1. After the second cone Player 2 decelerates and Player 1 accelerates again, this is repeated along the length of the grid (*see* fig. 7.14).

Key teaching points
- Both players should maintain correct running form/mechanics
- Both players should use a strong arm drive
- Both players should use short, explosive steps during the acceleration phase
- Player 2 (the assisted player) must keep an upright forward lean and not try to resist by leaning back as this will cause deceleration

Sets and reps
2 sets of 4 reps (each player completes 2 assisted and 2 resisted reps plus 1 contrast run per set). Players should take 20 seconds recovery between each rep and 3 minutes between each set.

Variations/progressions
- Players can run the grid with a stick
- Introduce a ball

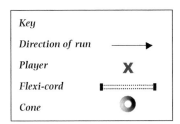

Key

Direction of run   ⟶

Player   **X**

Flexi-cord

Cone   ◯

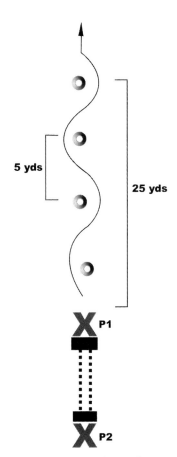

Figure 7.14 Assisted and resisted tow runs with serves

DRILL   *MAKING THE GOAL WIDER*

Aim

To encourage forward and midfield players to make well-timed runs on to the far post for what are often simple, 'tap in' goals.

Area/equipment

Indoor or outdoor area (for maximum benefit this drill should be performed in the relevant area of the pitch); Overspeed Tow Rope and cones set out to mark arcs of 20–30 yards long (*see* fig. 7.15).

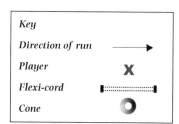

Description

Players 1 and 2 are connected by the Overspeed Tow Rope belts. Player 1 is assisted from the front and Player 2 resisted from the back. Player 3 holds the handle and provides different levels of overspeed. Player 1 will run the arc. Player 2 runs in a straight line away from Player 3 who moves back towards the original starting point of Player 1. (NB: It is vital that Player 3 carefully watches Player 1 to ensure that the correct level of overspeed/assistance is being provided.)

Key teaching points

■ Players 1 and 2 should maintain correct running form/mechanics
■ Player 1 should relax, go with the pull and not try to resist it
■ Player 2 should take short, fast steps
■ Player 3 must be very vigilant for the safety of Player 1

Sets and reps

After 1 rep rotate the players as follows: Player 2 (resisted) becomes Player 1 (assisted), Player 1 becomes Player 3 (support) and Player 3 becomes Player 2. Each player performs 5 reps in each role.

Variations/progressions

■ This is a very advanced drill! Introduce Player 4 who fires a ball in towards the far post for Player 1 to accelerate on to and deflect into the goal.
■ Perform the drill on the opposite (reverse stick) side.

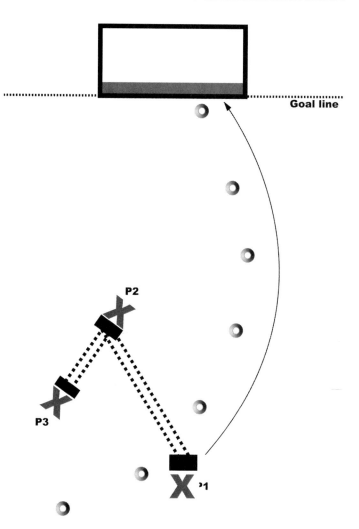

Figure 7.15 Making the goal wider

POSITION – FORWARDS
DRILL LEAD AND RE-LEAD

Aim
To develop a player's ability to lose a marker and to create and exploit space.

Area/equipment
Indoor or outdoor area; 1 Viper Belt, hockey balls and 3 cones set up as shown in fig. 7.16.

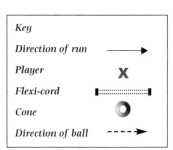

Description
Player 1 carries a stick and is connected to Player 2 by the Flexi-cord. Player 1 makes a 'lead' run to cone A, rolls around the cone and then accelerates (re-leads) towards cone C. As Player 1 moves between cones A and C, Player 3 feeds the ball on to their open stick side for Player 1 to receive, control and accelerate away for 3 yards. Return to the start position and repeat on the reverse stick side.

Key teaching points
- Player 1 must use good technique on receipt, control and acceleration away with the ball
- Quality passing from Player 3 is essential
- Players 1 and 3 must communicate well
- Good timing of runs and passes is essential

Sets and reps
2 sets of 10 (5 rolling to the left and 5 to the right) plus 2 contrast runs with a walk-back recovery between each rep and 3 minutes recovery between sets.

Variations/progressions
- Player 3 to vary the pass to Player 1 (lifted, random sides, etc.)
- Perform the drill near the circle area so that as Player 1 picks up the ball they are quickly into the circle for a shot – often off balance!
- Player 3 makes a support run after playing the pass and receives the ball back from Player 1

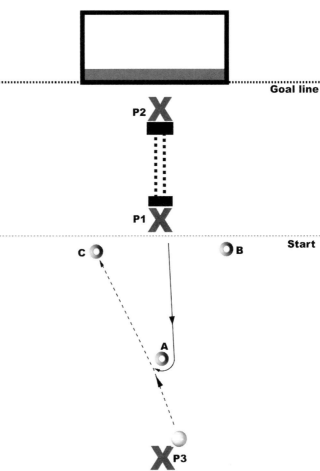

Figure 7.16 Lead and re-lead

123

DRILL   *EXPLOSIVE GROUND REACTION*

Aim
To develop multi-directional explosive movements.

Area/equipment
Indoor or outdoor hard-surfaced area; reaction ball.

Description
Players can work in pairs or against a wall. The reaction ball is thrown to land within 1 yard of the goalkeeper who attempts to catch it before the second bounce. Due to the shape of the ball it will bounce off the surface at different angles and different heights forcing the goalkeeper to react accordingly.

Key teaching points
- Bend at the knees, not at the waist
- Work off the balls of the feet
- Keep the hands in front of the body ready to react
- The ball should not be thrown hard – it will do the necessary work itself

Sets and reps
3 sets of 25 reps with 1 minute recovery between each set.

Variations/progressions
Vary the starting position of the goalkeeper, e.g. backwards, sideways, etc.

POSITION – GOALKEEPER

DRILL   *CLOSING DOWN AND COVERING ANGLES*

Aim
To improve the speed and efficiency of a goalkeeper when closing an attacking player down and narrowing his or her shooting angles.

Area/equipment
Indoor or outdoor area (for maximum benefit this drill should be performed in the relevant area of the pitch); Side-Steppers, cones and hockey balls.

Description
The goalkeeper stands in the middle of the goal wearing kit and a set of Side-Steppers. On the coach's call he or she explodes out to cone 1 then laterally to cone 2 or 3 as directed as though defending or moving with a player. As the goalkeeper reaches cone 3 the coach calls either 'baseline' (Y) – which represents a player tacking the ball to the baseline so that the goalkeeper moves to this position – or 'goal' (X) – which represents a player making a lifted shot so that the goalkeeper moves backwards from cone 3 to save a high ball thrown in by the coach.

Key teaching points
■ The goalkeeper should use explosive steps and arm drives when moving
■ Good goalkeeping techniques must be used in relation to holding the stick and making the saves
■ Keep the head and eyes up

Sets and reps
3 sets of 6 reps plus 2 contrast reps with 15 seconds recovery between each rep and 2 minutes between sets.

Variations/progressions
■ Instead of cones (1, 2 and 3) use a player or coach to whom the goalkeeper must respond
■ Vary the distances and angles that the goalkeeper works over
■ Use a Viper Belt as an alternative to Side-Steppers

Key	
Direction of run	→
Player	**X**
Cone	●
Coach	◉

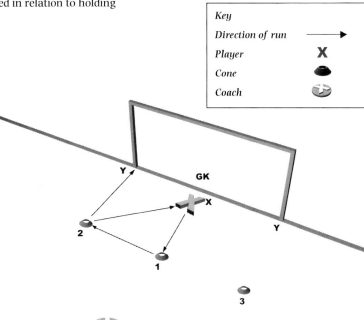

Figure 7.17 Closing down and covering angles

POSITION – GOALKEEPER

DRILL   *RESISTED SAVES*

Aim
To improve the speed and strength of goalkeepers' arm movements when making saves.

Area/equipment
Indoor or outdoor area (for maximum benefit this drill should be performed in the relevant area of the pitch); Side-Steppers and hockey balls.

Description
The goalkeeper, wearing kit, stands in the goal with a set of Side-Steppers attaching the wrists together. Holding the left hand to the chest, the goalkeeper makes resisted saves on the right side from balls being fed or thrown in by the coach.

Key teaching points
- Make sure that the left hand is kept as still as possible
- The feed for the save must be of high quality
- The goalkeeper must work off the balls of the feet

Sets and reps
3 sets of 20 reps (10 on the right side and 10 on the left) plus 4 contrasts with minimal recovery time between reps (goalkeeper to set the time), and 2 minutes recovery between each set.

Variations/progressions
- Use 2 punch/kick resisters as an alternative to Side-Steppers.
- Throw in some low feeds as well for the goalkeeper to make decisions on a leg or hand/arm save

DRILL | ***POSITION – GOALKEEPER***
RESISTED KICKS

Aim

To develop kicking power and better strength and distance on clearances.

Area/equipment

Indoor or outdoor area (for maximum benefit this drill should be performed in the relevant area of the pitch); Punch/Kick Resister and hockey balls placed randomly in the circle area.

Description

The goalkeeper, wearing kit, stands in the goal with a punch/kick resister attached to either foot. The goalkeeper then proceeds to clear all the hockey balls from the circle area ensuring that after each clearance he or she takes up a 'ready' stance in goal.

Key teaching points

- Goalkeepers should use correct kicking techniques
- Goalkeepers should clear to safe areas
- Small, controlled steps are to be used when moving back into the goal area
- Use both feet

Sets and reps

3 sets of 10 reps with minimal recovery time between reps (goalkeeper to set the time) and 2 minutes recovery between each set.

Variations/progressions

- Coach to feed balls in so the goalkeeper has to clear a moving ball
- Use Side-Steppers as an alternative, particularly for work over shorter distances

POSITION – GOALKEEPER

DRILL HORIZONTAL TO VERTICAL

Aim
To develop the explosive ability of the goalkeeper to go from a horizontal position to a vertical position in a controlled, efficient manner.

Area/equipment
Indoor or outdoor area (for maximum benefit this drill should be performed in the relevant area of the pitch); Viper Belt, Flexi-cord and cones.

Description
Player 1 (goalkeeper) wears the Viper Belt and is attached to Player 2 by the Flexi-cord. The coach nominates a cone 1–5, and on the call Player 1 accelerates to the cone, lies down as though making a save, gets up as quickly as possible to save a ball that has been fed in by the coach, before moving backwards into the goal to repeat the drill.

Key teaching points
- Goalkeeper must use correct techniques when lying down and making saves
- Goalkeeper should use short, explosive steps and a strong arm drive
- Work off the balls of the feet
- Player 2 should crouch down as Player 1 goes to the ground so that Player 1 feels resistance when getting up from the first-phase save
- Both sides should be worked equally

Sets and reps
2 sets of 6–8 reps with 15 seconds recovery between each rep and 2 minutes recovery between each set.

Variations/progressions
Goalkeeper reacts to visual signal rather than verbal

Key	
Player	**X**
Flexi-cord	I⋯⋯⋯I
Cone	●

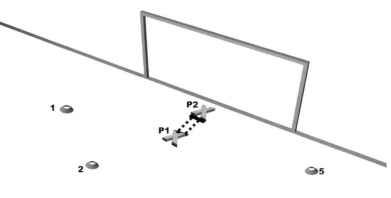

Figure 7.18 Horizontal to vertical explosion, second-phase save

DRILL | ### POSITION – GOALKEEPER
NARROWING THE ANGLE

Aim
To develop explosive acceleration, speed and agility over 5–10 yards, to improve the goalkeeper's ability to cut out crosses and close players down.

Area/equipment
Indoor or outdoor area (for maximum benefit this drill should be performed in the relevant area of the pitch); 4 short ladders and 7–8 cones positioned as shown in fig. 7.19.

Description
The goalkeeper, wearing kit, moves laterally along the goal line and then explodes down the ladder and onto the cone nominated by the coach. On arriving at the cone the goalkeeper makes a kick clearance or a diving save as instructed.

Key teaching points
- Goalkeeper must use correct techniques when diving and kicking, and in carrying the stick
- Use short, explosive steps and a strong arm drive
- Work off the balls of the feet
- Keep the head and eyes up

Sets and reps
2 sets of 6 reps with a walk-back recovery between each rep and 2 minutes recovery between each set.

Variations/progressions
- Introduce a ball that the goalkeeper has to kick clear or dive to clear
- The goalkeeper wears a Viper Belt and performs the drill under resistance (do not forget to perform a contrast)

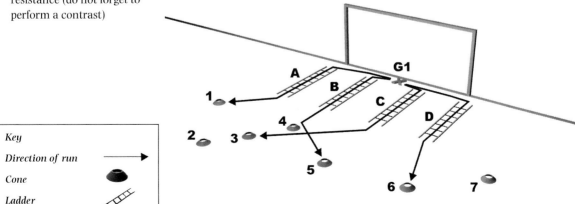

Figure 7.19 Narrowing the angle

POSITION – GOALKEEPER
LATERAL SPEED DEVELOPMENT

Aim
To develop fast, controlled lateral movement across the goalmouth.

Area/equipment
Indoor or outdoor area (for maximum benefit this drill should be performed in the relevant area of the pitch); 2 ladders and 8 hockey balls. Place the ladders just in front of and parallel to the goal line ensuring that there is a small gap between them where the goalkeeper will stand. Place the balls about 1–2 yards away from the ladder as shown in fig. 7.20.

Description
The goalkeeper stands in the space between the 2 ladders and performs a lateral fast-foot drill to the left or right as directed by the coach. The coach then nominates a ball that the goalkeeper explodes out of the ladder to clear.

Key teaching points
- Use strong arm drive when moving laterally and when exploding out of the ladder
- Use short, explosive steps
- Work off the balls of the feet
- Keep the head and eyes up
- Goal keeper must use both feet
- Goalkeeper should clear the balls to safe areas

Sets and reps
2 sets of 6 reps with a walk-back recovery between each rep and 2 minutes recovery between each set.

Variations/progressions
The goalkeeper wears a Viper Belt and performs the drill while resisted from both sides.

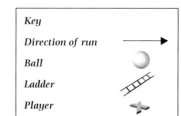

Key

Direction of run →

Ball

Ladder

Player

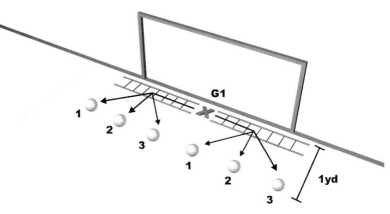

Figure 7.20 Lateral speed development

Due to the intense activity levels possible during the main part of the session, a warm-down should be performed gradually to bring the heart rate back to near resting levels. This will help to:

- disperse lactic acid

- prevent blood pooling in the lower body

- return the body systems to normal levels

- assist in recovery

The structure of the warm-down will essentially be the reverse of the Dynamic Flex warm-up and will last for approximately 5 minutes depending on the fitness level of the players. It begins with moderate Dynamic Flex movements. These will gradually become less intense and smaller in amplitude (like a warm-up in reverse). These exercises should still focus on quality of movement (good mechanics).

Static stretches should then be incorporated. Perform stretches that mirror the movements that are being carried out in the warm-down.

DRILL HIGH KNEE-LIFT SKIP

Follow the instructions given on page 9.

Aim
To warm down the hips and buttocks gradually.

Sets and reps
2 × 20 metres, 1 forwards and 1 backwards.

Intensity
60% for the first 20 yards and 50% for the second 20 yards.

DRILL KNEE-ACROSS SKIP

See instructions on page 6.

Aim
To warm down the hip flexors gradually by lowering the intensity of the exercise.

Sets and reps
2 × 20 yards, 1 forwards and 1 backwards.

Intensity
50% for the first 20 metres and 40% for the second.

DRILL WIDE SKIP

See instructions on page 8.

Aim
To warm down the hips and ankles.

Sets and reps
2 × 20 yards, 1 forwards and 1 backwards.

Intensity
40% for the first 20 yards and 30% for the second.

DRILL **CARIOCA**

See instructions on page 12.

Aim
To warm down the hips and the core.

Sets and reps
2 × 20 yards, 1 with the left leg leading and 1 with the right.

Intensity
30% for the first 20 yards and 20% for the second.

DRILL **SMALL SKIPS**

See instructions on page 5.

Aim
To warm down the muscles of the lower leg and ankle.

Sets and reps
2 × 20 yards, 1 forwards and 1 backwards.

Intensity
20% for the first 20 yards and 10% for the second.

DRILL **ANKLE FLICKS**

See instructions on page 4.

Aim
To bring the heart rate down and to stretch the calf and the ankle.

Sets and reps
2 × 20 yards, 1 forwards and 1 backwards.

Intensity
10% for the first 20 yards and walking flicks for the second.

DRILL HURDLE WALK

See instructions on page 16.

Aim
To bring the heart rate down.

Sets and reps
2 × 20 yards, 1 forwards and 1 backwards.

Intensity
Walking.

DRILL WALKING HAMSTRING

Aim
Back of thigh stretch.

Sets and reps
2 × 20 metres, 1 forwards and 1 backwards.

Intensity
Walking.

DRILL LATISSIMUS DORSI STRETCH

Aim
To stretch the muscles in the back.

Description
Stand in an upright position and link the hands together in front of the chest. Push the hands out and arch the back forwards simultaneously.

Key teaching points
- Do not force the arms out too far
- Focus on slow, controlled breathing

Sets and reps
Hold the stretch for about 10 seconds.

Intensity
Static.

DRILL | *QUADRICEPS STRETCH*

Aim
To stretch and assist the recovery of the thigh muscles.

Description
Stand on one leg and bring the heel of the raised foot in towards the buttock. Using the hand of that side, hold the instep and squeeze it into the buttock. Repeat on the other leg.

Key teaching points
- Try to keep the knees together
- Bend the support leg slightly
- Focus on slow, controlled breathing
- Do not force the stretch – just squeeze it in gently

Sets and reps
Hold the stretch for about 10 seconds on each leg.

Variation
The player can lie down sideways on the floor.

Intensity
Static.

DRILL | *HAMSTRING STRETCH*

Aim
To stretch and assist the recovery of the hamstring.

Description
Sit on the floor with one leg extended and the other leg bent. Bend forward from the hips and reach down towards the foot.

Key teaching points
- Focus on slow, controlled breathing
- Bend forwards from the hips
- Keep the back straight and flat
- Flex the foot to increase the stretch

Sets and reps
Hold the stretch for about 10 seconds on each leg.

Intensity
Static.

DRILL ADDUCTORS STRETCH

Aim
To stretch and assist the recovery of the adductor muscles.

Description
Stand with the legs apart, bend one knee and keep the foot at 45°, toes pointing ahead and knee over the ankle. The other leg should be straight. Repeat on the opposite leg.

Key teaching points
- Focus on slow, controlled breathing
- Do not force the stretch
- Keep the back straight
- Do not allow the knee of the bent leg to go beyond the toes

Sets and reps
Hold the stretch for about 10 seconds on each leg.

Intensity
Static.

DRILL CALF STRETCH

Aim
To stretch and assist the recovery of the calf muscles.

Area/equipment
Indoors or outdoors.

Description
Stand with the legs split and both feet pointing forwards, one leg to the front and the other to the back. The weight should be transferred to the front knee and then gently back. Repeat on the other leg. The back leg should be kept straight, it is this calf that will be stretched.

Key teaching points
- The front knee should move no further forward than above the ankle
- Focus on slow, controlled breathing
- Do not force the stretch
- Apply the weight slowly to the front foot

Sets and reps
Hold the stretch for about 10 seconds on each leg.

Intensity
Static.

CHAPTER 9 THE SAQ HOCKEY PROGRAMME

Modern hockey needs modern programmes that account for the speed and skill level and cater for individual positional needs. The most successful programmes are those that are varied, provide challenges, keep the players on their toes, accept individuality and are fun. Failing to provide a stimulating programme by including too much of the 'same' is guaranteed to demotivate players and squads, resulting in compromised performances in both training and games.

Some simple rules

- Start with dynamic flexibility

- Explosive work and sprints to be completed early in the session, before endurance work

- Plan sessions so that an explosive day is followed by a preparation day

- Progress from simple to complex drills

- Don't restrict programmes to one-week periods; work with different blocks of 4–8 to 10–12 days

- Acquire one new skill a day

- Rest and recovery periods must be well planned

- Vary work-to-rest ratios

- Build up strength before performing plyometrics

- Keep sessions short and sharp. Explanation and discussions should be conducted before and after, not in activity time

- Finish off each session with static stretching

Pre-season training

Mention pre-season training to most players and a look of horror will result. For years coaches and trainers have relied predominantly on the development of aerobic energy to prepare their players, often using, long, slow, steady-state runs of anything from 5 miles upwards.

Research clearly shows that this type of running is unsuitable for hockey players and, in fact, is more likely to cause unnecessary overuse injuries and – more importantly – to slow players down.

Hockey is a multi-directional, explosive, stop-start team game of 70 minutes' duration, although the ball is actually in play for less than half of this time. Most activity lasts for just a few seconds, with the average distance run per game phase being about 15–30 yards, depending on the game position of the player. Hockey uses fast-twitch fibres and therefore depends primarily on the anaerobic system, and a number of benefits are gained by training this system that impact on the overall level of fitness:

- an increased ability to tolerate higher levels of lactic acid – a by-product of high-intensity activity.

- an increase in aerobic power, which is the energy system that uses oxygen without 'turning off' the fast-twitch fibres – vital because it is these that enable players to perform explosive multi-directional movements such as sprinting, jumping, tackling and diving

- an improved recovery time – this is very important as it enables players to be ready more quickly for the next activity

Full–Time Programmes

There is an increasing number of elite hockey players who are able to train as full-time athletes. Not only does this allow for more training sessions on a weekly basis but it also allows the player the opportunity to develop stronger foundations more quickly. In particular the introduction of a well-structured weights programme will further enhance the effectiveness of the SAQ Programme.

As the season draws closer the emphasis progressively changes with a higher percentage of time being spent on the explosive development and less on the mechanics. By gradually shortening the recovery periods and increasing the intensity of the interval runs the programme becomes more game-like.

The in-season programmes are designed as a continuous top-up of the pre-season work, ensuring that players remain fresh, motivated and match-fit.

PRE–SEASON PROGRAMME – FULL–TIME

	A.M.	P.M.
MONDAY	Interval running	**SAQ Session:** mechanics and agility work Hockey skills session Flexibility Rest
TUESDAY	Weights Core stability work	Rest
WEDNESDAY	Interval running	**SAQ Session:** mechanics and agility work Hockey skills session Flexibility
THURSDAY	Weights Core stability work	Cross training – swimming, cycling, tennis, badminton, etc.
FRIDAY	Interval running	Rest
SATURDAY	Weights Core stability work	Cross training – swimming, cycling, tennis, badminton, etc.
SUNDAY	Rest	Rest

IN–SEASON PROGRAMME (with games on a Saturday)

	A.M.	P.M.
MONDAY	Weights Core work Flexibility	Team training to include SAQ session: emphasis on explosion
TUESDAY	Rest	Interval running
WEDNESDAY	Weights Core work Flexibility	Team training to include SAQ session: emphasis on explosion
THURSDAY	Interval running	Rest
FRIDAY	Core work Flexibility	Rest
SATURDAY	Game	Recovery stretching
SUNDAY	Active recovery	Rest

Part-Time Programmes

Around the world the majority of clubs that play hockey do so on a part-time basis. They normally train 2 or 3 times a week depending on the level of hockey that they play. The SAQ Hockey Programme can make training interesting, challenging and also great fun.

It is amazing how hard players work without realising it, and what good results will be achieved in all areas of their fitness. Do not fall into the trap of relying on steady-state runs. Interval running, SAQ hockey-specific drills and SAQ Hockey Circuits will help players become fitter and faster.

PRE-SEASON PROGRAMME – PART-TIME

All sessions start with Dynamic Flex

MONDAY	Weights or Jelly Ball Core work
TUESDAY	Interval running (longer) or cross training
WEDNESDAY	Weights or Jelly Ball Core work
THURSDAY	**SAQ Session:** Hockey Circuit
FRIDAY	Weights or Jelly Ball Core work
SATURDAY	**SAQ Session:** mechanics and agility work
SUNDAY	Rest

IN–SEASON PROGRAMME – PART–TIME

MONDAY	Interval running Core work
TUESDAY	Hockey skills session **SAQ Session:** mechanics and agility work
WEDNESDAY	Interval running Core work
THURSDAY	Hockey skills session **SAQ Session:** mechanics and agility work
FRIDAY	Rest
SATURDAY	Game Stretch
SUNDAY	Active recovery

References

Gleim, G.W. and McHugh, M.P. (1997), 'Flexibility and Its Effects on Sports Injury and Performance', *Sports Medicine*, 24(5): pp. 289–99.

Hennessy, L., Dr (2000), 'Developing Explosive Power', Paper, SAQ Symposium, June 2000.

Pope, R.C. (1999), 'Skip the Warm-Up', *New Scientist*, 18 Dec., 164: 23.

Smythe, R. (2000), 'Acts of agility', *Training & Conditioning*, 5(4): 22–5.

Index of drills